Replenishing the Earth

Also by Wangari Maathai

The Green Belt Movement:
Sharing the Approach and the Experience

Unbowed: A Memoir

The Challenge for Africa

Replenishing the Earth

Spiritual Values for

Healing Ourselves and the World

WANGARI MAATHAI

Doubleday

New York London Toronto Sydney Auckland

ŒD
DOUBLEDAY

Published in the United States by Doubleday Religion, an imprint
of the Crown Publishing Group, a division of
Random House, Inc., New York.

www.crownpublishing.com

DOUBLEDAY and the DD colophon are registered trademarks
of Random House, Inc.

All biblical quotations are taken from the New Revised Standard
Version of the Bible. Iowa Falls, Iowa: World Bible Publishers, Inc.,
copyright © 1989.

Library of Congress Cataloging-in-Publication Data

Maathai, Wangari.
Replenishing the earth: spiritual values for healing ourselves and the
world / Wangari Maathai. — 1st ed.
p. cm.
Includes bibliographical references (p.) and index.
1. Human ecology — Religious aspects 2. Human ecology
3. Spiritual healing. I. Title.
BT695.5.M315 2010
261.8'8 — dc22   2010009034

ISBN 978-0-307-59114-2

Printed in the United States of America

Design by Leonard W. Henderson

10 9 8 7 6 5 4 3 2 1

First Edition

Behold my works! See how beautiful they are, how excellent! All that I have created for your sake did I create it. See to it that you do not spoil and destroy my world; for if you do, there will be no one to repair it after you.

—Ecclesiastes Rabbah 7:13

For my granddaughter, Ruth Wangari

Contents

Introduction	13
1: Beginnings	27
2: The Wounds	37
3: Changing Perspectives	57
4: The Power of the Tree	77
5: Sacred Groves, Sacred No More	93
6: Gratitude and Respect	105
7: Self-Empowerment	131
8: Self-Knowledge	143
9: The Commitment to Service	157
10: Spirituality Meets Activism	171
11: Responding to the Call to Serve	183
Acknowledgments	197
Notes	201

Replenishing the Earth

Introduction

During my more than three decades as an environmentalist and campaigner for democratic space, people have often asked me whether spirituality, different religious traditions, and the Bible in particular inspired me and influenced my activism and the work of the Green Belt Movement (GBM). Did I conceive conservation of the environment and empowerment of ordinary people as a kind of religious experience or vocation? Are there, people asked, spiritual lessons to be learned and applied to environmental efforts, or to life as a whole?

Upon reflection, it is clear to me that when I began this work in 1977, I wasn't motivated by my faith or by religion in general. Instead, the motivation came from thinking literally and practically about how to solve problems on the ground. It was a desire to help rural populations, especially women, with the basic needs they described to me during seminars and workshops. They said that they lacked clean drinking water, adequate and nutritious food, income, and enough energy for cooking and heating. So, when these questions were asked during the early days, I'd answer that I didn't think digging holes and mobilizing communities to protect or restore the trees, forests, watersheds, soil, or habitats for wildlife that surrounded them was spiritual work or only relevant to the religious.

Personally, however, I never differentiated between activities that might be called "spiritual" and those that might be termed "secular." After a few years I came to recognize that our efforts weren't only about planting trees, but were also about sowing seeds of a different sort—the ones necessary to heal the wounds inflicted on communities that robbed them of their self-confidence and self-knowledge. What became clear was that individuals within these communities had to rediscover their authentic voice and speak out on behalf of their rights (human, environmental, civic, and political). Our task also became to expand democratic space in which ordinary citizens could make decisions on their own behalf to benefit themselves, their community, their country, and the environment that sustains them.

In this context, I began to appreciate that there *was* something that inspired and sustained the GBM and those participating in its activities over the years. Many people from different communities and regions reached out to the GBM because they wanted to share the approach and the experience. In time, I came to realize that the work of the GBM was driven not only by passion and vision but also by certain intangible core values.

The Four Core Values of the Green Belt Movement

1. **Love for the environment:** Such a love is demonstrable in one's lifestyle. It motivates one to take positive actions for the earth, such as plant trees and ensure that they survive; nurture those trees that are stand-

ing; protect animals and their habitats; conserve the soil; and undertake other such activities that show appreciation in a tangible way for the earth and the immediate environment and all they provide.

2. **Gratitude and respect for Earth's resources:** This entails valuing all that the earth gives us, and because of that valuation, not wanting to waste any of it, and therefore practicing the three R's: reduce, reuse, recycle. In Japan, the term used for this concept is *mottainai.*

3. **Self-empowerment and self-betterment:** This is the desire to improve one's life and life circumstances through the spirit of self-reliance, and not wait for someone else to do it for you. It also entails turning away from inertia and self-destructive activities such as addictions. It encompasses the understanding that the power to change is within you, as is the capacity to provide oneself with the inner energy that's needed.

4. **The spirit of service and volunteerism:** This value, which is at the forefront of the Green Belt Movement's work, means using one's time, energy, and resources to provide service to others, without expecting or demanding compensation, appreciation, or even recognition. It is the giving of self that characterizes prophets, saints, and many local heroes. It puts a priority on doing one's part to achieve the common good: both for those who are near and dear and for strangers who may be in faraway places. "Others" should also include nonhumans, with whom we share life and the planet.

These values encapsulate the intangible, subtle, nonmaterial-istic aspects of the GBM as an organization. Without them, I'm convinced the organization couldn't have survived and thrived, because many of the labors were never undertaken for money, fame, or advancement, and certainly not with the expectation of someday being awarded a Nobel Peace Prize! At times, the work brought much misery and weariness. But due to our embracing these values—as well as a commitment to embody justice, equity, responsibility, and accountability—persistence became our trademark: through our campaigns, and in our interactions with communities, elected officials, re-ligious leaders, activists, and even heads of state.

Such values are not unique to the Green Belt Movement. They are universal, but they can't be touched or seen. We can-not place a monetary value on them: in effect, they are price-less. They define our humanity.

These values are not contained only within certain reli-gious traditions. Neither does one have to profess a faith in a divine being to live by them. However, they do seem to be part of human nature, and I'm convinced that we are better people because we hold them, and that humankind is better off with them than without them. Where these values are ignored, they are replaced by vices such as selfishness, corruption, greed, and exploitation, and can even lead to death.

Through experience and observation, I have come to real-ize that the physical destruction of the earth extends to human-ity, too. If we live in an environment that's wounded—where the water is polluted, the air is filled with soot and fumes, the food is contaminated with heavy metals and plastic residues, or the soil is practically dust—it hurts us, chipping away at our health and creating injuries at a physical, psychological, and spiritual level. In degrading the environment, therefore, we degrade ourselves and all humankind.

The reverse is also true. In the process of helping the earth to heal, we help ourselves. If we see the earth bleeding from the loss of topsoil, biodiversity, or drought and desertification, and if we help reclaim or save what is lost—for instance, through regeneration of degraded forests—the planet will help us in our self-healing and indeed survival. When we can eat healthier, nonadulterated food; when we can breathe clean air and drink clean water; when the soil can produce an abundance of vegetables and grains, our own sicknesses and unhealthy lifestyles become healed. The same values we employ in the service of the earth's replenishment work for us, too. We can love ourselves by loving the earth; feel grateful for who we are, even as we are grateful for the earth's bounty; better ourselves, even as we use that self-empowerment to improve the earth; offer service to ourselves, even as we practice volunteerism for the earth.

Human beings have a consciousness by which we can appreciate love, beauty, creativity, and innovation or mourn the lack thereof. To the extent that we can go beyond ourselves and ordinary biological instincts, we can experience what it means to be human and therefore different from other forms of life. We can appreciate the delicacy of dew or a flower in bloom, water as it runs over the pebbles, or the majesty of an elephant, the fragility of the butterfly, or a field of wheat or leaves blowing in the wind. Such aesthetic responses are valid in their own right, and as reactions to the natural world they can inspire in us a sense of wonder and beauty that in turn encourages a sense of the divine.

That consciousness acknowledges that while a certain tree, forest, or mountain itself may not be holy, the life-sustaining services it provides—the oxygen we breathe, the water we drink—are what make existence possible, and so deserve our respect. From this point of view, the environment becomes sacred, because to destroy what is essential to life is to destroy life itself. Likewise, the spiritual values explored in this book are closely linked with nature. Many prophets from various religious traditions were inspired by nature or withdrew into it to tap its wisdom. In addition, we humans often don't have the vocabulary to express our thoughts and ideas about the numinous, so we use symbols, many of which we find in the natural world, such as the tree, river, sun, moon, and animals.

Indeed, it's because of this connection that people who are religious should be closest to the planet and in the forefront of recognizing that it needs healing. Unfortunately, many of us have become detached from the natural world through industrialization, mechanization, urbanization, and habitat loss. The original ideas and thoughts of the founders of religions and traditions were distorted or modified to suit the customs of people who embraced them. As a result, over time the followers became distant from what was initially conveyed by the founders. In the Christian tradition, for example, aspects of the original faith were disconnected from care of the earth, when carriers of the faith became politically entangled with the expansionists, colonialists, and exploiters of peoples and the planet. They at once facilitated and created the wounds that need to be healed today.

In *Replenishing the Earth*, I explore the broader application of the core values that continue to guide the Green Belt Movement and that remain at the center of its activities, wherever the spirit of the movement is embraced. These values must be more widely embraced if we are to heal the myriad wounds that have been inflicted on the planet and subsequently on ourselves. I am neither a theologian nor a student of religions or faith traditions. Therefore, this book should not be read as a theological statement or moral guideline for environmentalists. The values I explore here are not exhaustive: rather, they are those that have been most relevant in my own life and work. They are not commonplace, and members of the Green Belt Movement, both new and old, are constantly reminded about them.

The book is divided into three parts. In the first part (chapters 1 and 2), I explore the relevance of the core values and describe how they became central to the work of the Green Belt Movement and, to an extent, my life, too. Then I relate a long journey that culminates with a trip I made into the Congo rain forest that illustrates many of the earth's wounds. These are the external conditions of our damaged world that impact not only the environment in which we live but also what we might call our inner ecology, our soul and sense of being human. Our first task must be to acknowledge these wounds, something that is at once simple and, because some of these wounds are so deep, immeasurably difficult.

Sometimes, in order to see clearly, we need to step aside and look at a situation from different perspectives. In chapter 3, the second part of this book, I enumerate three ways of looking at our planet. The first is the big picture, using the vision of Earth from space that has been available to us since man landed on the moon. The second is a simple but long view of Earth's history over the eons. The third is the picture of Earth we receive when we concentrate on the local and the small. Each of these perspectives helps us to shift our consciousness and make us aware of our relative position within the cosmos and the fact that we are a part of, not apart from, all that exists.

The third part of *Replenishing the Earth*, from chapters 4 through 11, examines the relevance of the four core values of the Green Belt Movement to our everyday actions, whether we live in Africa or elsewhere. Even though my life experiences have led me to an ecumenical understanding of faith, in Kenya, as in much of Africa south of the Sahara, Christianity is the dominant religion and the Bible is usually the only text that people associate with it. Therefore, in the GBM's efforts to reach out to local communities we use the Bible, and as a result, many of the examples are drawn from what to Christians are known as the Old and New Testaments. These teachings offer guidance — alas, widely ignored by the faithful — on how the earth's natural resources ought to be treated. I also explore in these chapters other faiths and spiritual traditions that indicate a reverence or respect for the natural world and that suggest ways of acknowledging the earth's wounds and working to heal them.

In tandem with the Judeo-Christian heritage, throughout *Replenishing the Earth* I illustrate some of the themes with examples from the traditional practices of the Kikuyu community, to which I belong and in which I was raised. Its worldview is generally representative of many native and indigenous communities, or micro-nations, and is the tradition with which I am most familiar. Although this worldview was considered "primitive" by Christian missionaries, the mores and values of traditional societies were not necessarily in conflict with the "new" or "modern" religious doctrines, which promised enlightenment, wealth, and happiness, especially in the afterlife. Sadly, however, the missionaries judged native rituals and ceremonies incompatible with the new faiths. Therefore, these practices were often demonized or eventually destroyed, with the full participation of the natives themselves. This was especially tragic because scientists are beginning to recognize that these traditional cultures and their lifestyles were responsible for the conservation of rich biodiversity in their environments. Therefore, many people — both scientists and laypersons — are finding it both self-evident and worthwhile to revisit the beliefs of native peoples to try to learn what they can from them before they vanish altogether.

My layperson's understanding of the divine is very limited, and although throughout this book the word "God" is used to describe the monotheistic deity of the Abrahamic traditions (Judaism, Christianity, and Islam) and the Kikuyu, I also use the term "the Source." Such a term helps remove the image that retains a hold over many Christians of a kindly grandfather sitting in heaven watching over all things and controlling our destinies. In this sense, then, the Source is the place of all knowledge and awareness. It is the repository of all that we cannot explain: which some call God, some Nature, and some the Creator. Although different cultures have different names for this originating energy—what the ancient Greeks called the Alpha and the Omega—and some may be unwilling to give it a name at all, who will claim that there is no Source or deny that in some way we are not all forms of energy?

In this conception, the Source is not in the business of fixing the mistakes of those who are careless or ignorant. If farmers overgraze their land, encourage desertification by cutting down trees, tolerate soil erosion, or don't harvest rainwater, then it's not God's fault when there is a drought and humans face the adverse consequences. One is left to wonder whether conceiving of God as the origination of all that is would make people of faith recognize that they have a responsibility to be the custodians of God's creation and, in the process, their own survival.

Even though God is the Source, there is not a limitless provision of all that our hearts desire. When a well is dug in the village or a river flows nearby, too many faithful believe blindly that the Source will provide that water forever. But the river or the wellspring can run dry, and what we thought of as something without need of replenishment is depleted. Our capacity as human beings to understand limits, to recognize that the planet we live on has finite natural capital, is failing to keep up with science. The lifestyles of the relatively rich, and the ever-increasing numbers of people wanting the material goods that come with those lifestyles, are placing enormous strains on the ecosystems on which that wealth depends.

Scientists, climate specialists, and others are alerting us that we have limited time to start making serious attempts to mitigate the effects of climate change. The Intergovernmental Panel on Climate Change (IPCC) estimates that by 2100, the global temperature is set to climb significantly, by between 1.8°C (3.2°F) at the low end and 4°C (7.2°F) at the high end. Sea levels are expected to rise by the end of this century by between 11 and 17 inches, threatening small island states.[1] Extreme weather events such as droughts, floods, heat waves, and hurricanes have increased in frequency and this trend is expected to continue as the climate becomes less predictable.

Africa is expected to be particularly hard-hit by climate change, with temperature rises of 0.2°C (0.4°F) per decade to 0.5°C (0.9°F) per decade. Warming will be most intense along the semiarid margins of the Sahara and in central southern Africa. Under the high estimate of possible warming, large parts of Africa would experience significant variability in seasonal rains, which could mean more frequent droughts, failed harvests, flooding, and more desertification. In addition, according to the IPCC, "There is wide consensus that climate change, through increased extremes, will worsen food security [in Africa]."[2]

Climate change is forcing all of us—rich and poor—to acknowledge that we have reached a point in the evolution of this planet where our needs and wants are outstripping the ability of the earth to provide, and that some of us will have to do with less if those who have very little are going to have enough to survive. It may require a conscious act of some of us saying no in addition to finding other, less destructive ways to say yes.

We do not know exactly what will happen, or where, in the coming century as the effects of climate change become evident. Computer models forecast that storms, droughts, and other catastrophic weather events will get more frequent and more intense. According to such models it is also highly possible that rising sea levels will flood low-lying areas of the planet, including those with dense human populations, forcing millions of people to move en masse inland or take to the open water in huge flotillas of refugees. It seems probable that more uncertain harvests and pressures on scarce natural resources will make conflict between peoples (whether displaced or otherwise) more common. Indeed, we are already seeing this in Sudan, East Africa, and elsewhere. The industrialized countries may have the technological and financial means to deal with the worst of the upheavals, but most of the more than five billion (and rising) people who live in the less industrialized world currently do not.

None of the healing that is necessary is automatic; it will require much work, for the wounds that have been created in the earth are deep. If we can't or won't assist in the earth's healing process, the planet might not take care of us either. As the scientist James Lovelock has hypothesized (conceiving the planet as Gaia, a vast, interconnected organism in its own right), the earth will find ways to return to thermal equilibrium by whatever regulatory means it can. But we and other species may be the losers if we cannot adapt fast enough. The questions we have to ask ourselves are these: Will we have the foresight now to stop the worst from happening, or will we wait until it is too late? We have the power to guide the earth toward a goal that's beneficial for our own goals, too. Will we adjust our practices and values in time to stop our own destruction?

These questions insist on more than merely a scientific answer, which is why the ecological crisis is both a physical crisis and a spiritual one. Addressing it requires a new level of consciousness, where we understand that we belong to the larger family of life on Earth. If we were able to achieve this consciousness, we'd see that the planet is hurting, and internalize the spiritual values that can help us move to address the wounds. We'd recognize that it should be in our nature to be custodians of the planet and do what's right for the earth and, in the process, for ourselves.

CHAPTER ONE

Beginnings

Within a few years of its inception in 1977, the Green Belt Movement (GBM) expanded from a small, tree-planting project at the National Council of Women of Kenya to a full-time engagement. Simultaneously, a small number of community groups grew to a network of thousands of such groups. As this occurred, it became clear that both the groups and the individuals were not upholding standards of behavior that they expected of others, especially those in government, which was already much criticized. These standards included honesty, hard work, and a commitment to transparency and accountability. It gradually became clear that the Green Belt Movement's work with communities to repair the degraded environment could not be done effectively without participants embracing a set of core spiritual values.

Therefore, it became necessary to raise awareness of issues of governance and the management of resources. Consequently, these values—love for the environment, gratitude and respect for the earth's resources, self-empowerment and self-betterment, and the spirit of service and volunteerism—emerged as a central feature of what we came to call "civic and environmental education." These comprised a set of seminars that we held for those wanting to participate in the work of the movement so they could know the procedures and values that should guide them. The seminars were designed to deepen individuals' understanding of the root causes of ecological destruction and the role political management of resources can play in the breakdown of the environment. Participants were encouraged to delve into why their environment was degraded, and the role that they and other members of their communities and society at large play in this.

At each seminar, each group enumerates its problems. It is then challenged to explore where those problems came from and how to develop a set of actions it can take to solve them both immediately and in the long term—at individual, household, and community levels, and on a small or larger scale. While many people may see a reason to plant trees to meet their own basic needs, the idea of creating a clean and healthy environment that may benefit everyone rather than only individuals is new. During the seminars, women and men who have been passive about environmental issues around them become self-empowered and energized to take action. They embrace the idea of being willing to work for something larger than themselves. When they return to their homes, they become eager to report how many tree seedlings they have nurtured in tree nurseries, how many trees they've planted, and how many people they've talked to in their local assemblies, including churches, about their newfound interest. For many GBM members, their satisfaction in their own efforts means that even the small financial compensation they receive for each tree seedling that survives becomes the token it is intended to be, rather than a formal payment for the work done.

Their circle of concern expands beyond themselves and encompasses the common good.

Those who embrace the values at the heart of the seminars — love for the environment, gratitude and respect for the earth's resources, self-empowerment and self-betterment, the spirit of service and volunteerism — remain involved in tending tree nurseries, transplanting seedlings, and restoring landscapes and indigenous forests. They also engage in other GBM activities such as collecting rainwater, terracing their fields to stem soil erosion, and planting food crops in their gardens to improve food security for their households. They also are involved in building and maintaining low-tech sand dams to ensure water supplies in the dry season. And, moreover, they stand up and advocate for their rights to a clean and healthy environment.

In the beginning of the work with the Green Belt Movement, it surprised me that many individuals and groups did not practice these spiritual values as part of their faith. By then, almost everybody was a Christian and these values are deeply entrenched in Christian teachings. I'd had them transmitted to me first by parents, then by teachers, friends, members of my community, and associates. My mother was always working hard, and I helped her in ways that now I can hardly believe. Even though I was very young, I cultivated food crops in the field, gathered firewood, fetched water from a nearby stream, went to the market, and ran many errands for her. I took care of my young siblings, and on one memorable occasion carried home a huge harvest of red kidney beans that was too heavy even for our family's donkey. My father, too, worked hard as a mechanic on a British settler's farm and supported a large family.

As I was growing up, I also learned that my grandparents' generation had maintained a proud heritage that had a strong commitment to justice, sense of right and wrong, and a belief in honesty. They didn't have to learn these values; they were simply passed along as an inheritance, very early in life. When children are exposed to values, and they see them embraced by those around them in their actions, the values become part of their personalities and are hard to unlearn.

At school, I was encouraged to be honest, too, and I was lucky to possess a mental attitude that was not constrained by judgment or religious dogmas. Catholic nuns—first the Consolata sisters from Italy, then the Irish Loreto nuns, and finally the Benedictine sisters of Mount St. Scholastica College in the United States—taught me from the age of twelve. They encouraged my curiosity, an embrace of the scientific method, and the use of critical thinking. Such exposure made it easy for me to listen and assess without prejudgments, and this has assisted me greatly in my life journey.

Today, people often ask me how I determined all those decades ago that the environment was so important. To a certain extent it was not my discovery. I was led by events that were happening around me at the time. For example, in 1972, the United Nations held its first global conference on the environment in Stockholm, Sweden. In 1973, the UN Environment Programme (UNEP) was established in Nairobi, with Maurice Strong as its first executive director. I was invited to join a group that established the Environmental Liaison Center International, a nongovernmental (nonprofit) environmental organization founded to work closely with UNEP and monitor its activities.

As I gained knowledge from others who knew much more than I did then, I became interested. This enabled me to respond when, in the lead-up to the first UN women's conference in Mexico City in 1975, I listened to rural women in Kenya listing their problems. I could see that all the challenges they had were rooted in a degraded rural environment. Planting trees came to me as a concrete, doable response.

I came to identify trees as the answer to the environmental problems the Kenyan women faced, partly because I grew up in the countryside surrounded by trees and green vegetation. But I was also fortunate at the time to be involved with organizations that were becoming aware of this issue. I can also point to the Source as the wellspring for all of the ideas that came.

Sometimes the inspiration to act arrives as a spark; sometimes it takes the form of a process. Whether one is drawn into an action through a sudden rush of inspiration, or through the slow dawning of a realization that something needs to change, I would argue that it all comes from the Source. But it's nonetheless essential to cultivate an attitude that allows you to take advantage of that awakening. This entails keeping your mind, eyes, and ears open, so that when an idea arrives you'll be ready for it. To be able to capitalize on our inspiration it is also important to be predisposed to welcome new sets of knowledge and retain an open mind. We need to appreciate as much as possible that a further horizon always lies beyond the one we see in front of us; there are always opportunities to learn and to examine one's own perception in light of recent information or revelations.

Ideas, it would seem, are like fruits hanging from trees: when they're ripe, you have to be ready to catch them before they fall. Like the five wise virgins of Jesus' parable (see Matt. 25:1–13), we must seize the opportunities presented to us, by making sure that we're fully prepared with the appropriate mental, physical, and spiritual capacity to take on the challenge. The environment must be ripe.

Sometimes such an awakening comes in the process of work or engagement in a cause or a joint effort. You realize how important something is—as I did with the environment—and you begin moving from working by yourself to communicating its importance to others. Before long, almost before you realize it, you have many people working with you.

When I told the rural women about the benefits of trees—that they'd help stem soil erosion and improve the health of the soil, making it possible to grow healthy foods; that they'd provide firewood, fodder for livestock, and shade; that they'd help regulate rainfall and provide a habitat for small animals and birds—I discovered that I'd opened a Pandora's box. In trying to solve one environmental problem, I found there were many other problems that the women and their communities needed to solve.

When I began the civic and environmental seminars, I didn't imagine that the core values at the center of the Green Belt Movement's work would be in such short supply! Without the value of volunteerism, the organization's work would not be sustainable, because we have never been flush with funds. It's impossible to compensate people for every bit of work they do; a price tag cannot and should not be placed on everything we do for the environment. And that is the way it was traditionally, before the cash economy arrived in Kenya: individuals had a profound sense that they must give back to their communities by providing voluntary service for the common good. The farther people moved away from traditional life and became "modern," the less willing they were to serve. Everything had to be paid for, and those who couldn't pay were pushed out.

This modern deficit in values existed in every aspect of society: within the government, from which we received not only indifference but often outright hostility; among the public, who couldn't believe that anybody, including members of the Green Belt Movement, would be working so hard solely for the common good. Each assumed that we must have an ulterior motive, such as money, or power, or political advantage—not least because there seemed to be no good reason why we would *not* be practicing the vices that brought money, power, or political advantage and patronage. No one seemed to realize that such vices—which included selfishness, greed, and the exploitation of the available resources—would cause harm that would eventually affect everyone. This deep disconnection from others and the environment would come back to haunt the same society.

When the women came to the GBM and complained that they didn't have enough firewood to cook healthy food for their children, naysayers couldn't argue that trees were *not* a practical response. What they wondered was why I made it *my* business to work with them and find a solution. When I explained how important it was not to deforest Kenya's main water catchment areas and not to plant the wrong type of tree along the riverbanks, in forests, or in wetlands, it was self-evident that a severe problem—water and soil erosion—

was being addressed. What detractors questioned was why *I* should be concerned about it.

"Don't you have anything better to do with your education?" some people asked. After all, as I was part of a small, educated elite within Kenyan society, someone who'd been a professor at the University of Nairobi, it was expected that I should be in the classroom dealing with academic matters rather than in the fields persuading rural women to plant trees. But I wasn't alone digging holes! Many other women were planting trees with me and were also expending considerable effort for something more than material compensation and personal gain. They, too, must have been motivated by a set of values and not just responding to their basic needs and individual gratification.

Since its beginning, the Green Belt Movement has moved from the simple act of tree-planting to meet immediate needs to attempting to mitigate the effects of climate change and heal the earth's wounds. When it started undertaking advocacy on matters of governance and rights, challenging those in power who were destroying the environment and putting citizens in danger in the process, some people may have thought it was silly, or foolhardy. Sometimes I wasn't sure myself why I continued. I knew, though, that the work wasn't being done for any ulterior motive, and that the GBM was addressing serious issues. I became even more certain that what we were doing was right, because we were dealing with basic and viable solutions to real and chronic problems. Experiences fed on themselves, and propelled participants and the work to the next level. Serving for the common good might be taxing or even dangerous at times, but the Source and the values are strong forces that kept us moving forward.

In time, individuals from outside of Kenya (principally Europe and the United States) reached out and wanted to support the GBM's work financially. They did this not because they wanted participants to gain personally, but because they wanted to do something good for the environment and the people living in the region. They recognized that we needed to protect our environment, but poverty was widespread. When I found myself in trouble with the Kenyan government, a number of people put their lives on the line to help me. Why did they bother, even though they were not next of kin, members of the same ethnic group, or my countrymen? It was because, like many others in the world, they were not driven by selfishness, the need to control others, or the desire to accumulate more. They were motivated by compassion, empathy, and recognition that the environment needs to be protected everywhere and that this is a matter of global concern to all.

Through this combination of questions about motivations, the development of the civic and environmental seminars, and my work in the field with Green Belt Movement groups, I've been encouraged to search more deeply into the issue of spiritual values. I've sought to understand whether those driven by such values are being stupid or naïve, or both, for wanting to work for the common good and expecting others to do the same. I've been challenged to ask myself why this set of values should be important for society, how these values might make a difference in our lives, and whether those of us who embody them are the fools or the wise ones.

CHAPTER TWO

The Wounds

In early 2009, I joined a small group of concerned individuals, a government minister, and members of the press on a fact-finding visit to a program run by a timber company active in the Republic of the Congo to ascertain whether it was a model of what could be called sustainable forestry management.

Four years earlier, in 2005, the ten countries that contain parts of the Congo Basin rain forest in central Africa had invited me to be the ecosystem's goodwill ambassador. The Congo Basin is an area of 700,000 square miles, some fifty million people, and tens of thousands of species of flora and fauna. My responsibility would be to help raise the profile of the region: its biodiversity and the significant role it is believed to play in regulating the planet's climate. I readily agreed, since I'd seen for myself how vital forests were to human communities and other forms of life that dwell in them.

Scientists call the Congo Basin's forest the world's "second lung," after the Amazon, because of the sheer volume of carbon dioxide it absorbs and the oxygen it exhales. Keeping this ecosystem healthy and using the resources it contains in a manner that's both sustainable and equitable without destroying it are not merely of concern for central Africa, but for the continent at large. Without the Congo forest, Africa would be one huge desert. It needs to be protected.

Our small group caught a plane from the Republic of the Congo's capital, Brazzaville, and flew for hours north and then east, over mile upon mile of dense greenery. We arrived at a landing strip in Pokola, a small town not far from the border with Cameroon. A representative of the timber company met us and explained that they'd been harvesting trees in the region for more than twenty years. He pointed to an area that had been logged about a decade earlier. I could see by the amount of vegetation and the number and height of the trees that, at least in this one segment, the forest had been able to regenerate itself.

From there, the group boarded two boats and traveled up the Sangha, a tributary of the vast Congo River. The Sangha was wider than an average four-lane street in any city, with dark, clear, placid waters that meandered silently through the forest. When I was a child, the streams where I grew up in Kenya's Central Highlands were narrow, fast moving, and clear. The water made a whooshing noise as it hurtled over the stones of the riverbed. However, too often these days, deforestation has caused siltation of many rivers, and the waters themselves have become so shallow they barely whisper over the pebbles. Indeed, sometimes the beds dry out altogether. The Sangha was a stark contrast, and a pleasant one—broad, unmuddied, and full of water.

After about an hour on the river, we came to an opening in the forest where we alighted from the boat. We were greeted by local residents, including Aka pygmies, who live in the forest, and others from Bantu communities (a group of peoples in east and southern Africa related by language that comprise the majority of the continent's population). As the people clapped and sang in welcome, I joined them to express my appreciation and gratitude, even though I didn't understand their words. What required no translator, however, was the evidence that in spite of the joy on their faces these people were very poor. Their clothes were in tatters, and their drawn faces and thin bodies showed signs of a hard life in the forest.

Our host, the timber company representative, wanting to demonstrate the aspects of the business that were socially and environmentally responsible, took us to a site where the company had, he said, worked with the Aka to protect trees important to their culture or for food. While I was pleased to see this sensitivity, the area of forest being saved was small compared to the area being logged. However, the local community appeared happy with the effort to conserve trees that were important to their culture and lifestyle.

The company was also anxious to show us how their workers felled trees selectively and sustainably. We were given crash helmets, and then turned our attention to a large sapele tree, about seventy feet tall and perhaps eight feet in diameter, with roots that fanned out from the base and anchored themselves firmly in the ground. The canopy of the tree was broad, shaped like an umbrella, and filled with smallish, dark green leaves.

An overseer instructed ten or so men with chain saws to cut it so it fell in a particular direction and didn't crush other, younger trees that were growing. This concern for the other trees also impressed me. For ten or fifteen minutes we watched as the men sawed. Finally, the tree swayed and fell to the ground with a huge bang that seemed to reverberate across the entire forest.

Our host told us that the tree almost certainly had been more than two centuries old. Two hundred years! I thought. For all we knew, it might have survived for another two centuries: retaining water and anchoring soil throughout its root system, storing carbon and releasing oxygen, and providing a home for birds, numerous insects, beetles, and other species in its trunk and canopy. Certainly, the fact that it had taken saws several minutes to bring the sapele to the ground showed that it was not ready to come down, not ready to loosen its tenacious grip on the soil, and not ready to stop providing environmental services.

As I watched the tree fall, tears welled in my eyes. The timber company representative noticed that I had become emotional. "Don't worry," he said. "There are millions of other trees out there in the forest."

This seemed small comfort. As we walked back to where we'd embarked, I asked the representative how much of the sapele would become timber. Thirty-five percent was the reply. I was surprised at how little that was, and inquired why the other 65 percent wasn't processed and shipped overseas, or transported to Brazzaville, Kinshasa, or even Nairobi, cities where it would be valuable and much sought after. Our host answered that this wasn't logistically possible or financially viable. Besides, he added, unless other logging companies operating in the Congo were required to process and export more or all of the trees they cut, his company's importation and use of the needed technology would put it at a financial disadvantage. Nevertheless, for the sake of the environment the company was planning to begin using this technology within the next three years. How would they do it competitively?

I didn't have to wait long to find out what happened to the 65 percent of the sapele. Our group was taken to another site, where Vietnamese workers were feeding the remainder of the tree into a hot kiln where bricks were being made. Those bricks would be used to build houses nearby for the timber company's workers. The local people took the rest of the wood and turned it into charcoal, which was used as fuel both locally and in distant towns and cities. Thick smoke and ash blanketed the area. I felt it in my throat and eyes.

What I saw that day felt like a wound on many levels. What stung me most was the waste involved in the transformation of that two-hundred-year-old sapele. Instead of turning the tree into fodder for the kiln, the timber company could have constructed their workers' houses from the lumber itself. The local people didn't use bricks to construct their homes, nor did they have the knowledge or technology to make bricks. Workers from abroad had to come to the Congo to do the work instead. Bricks, of course, aren't essential for dwellings. But homes made from them are seen as modern and progressive in much of Africa, and thus are desired. (Most Africans don't know that houses built of wood in developed countries have stood for hundreds of years.) The company had obviously conceded to public opinion and decided that its workers wouldn't live in wood houses, or those constructed of more traditional materials such as mud and straw. They would build brick houses even if they had to import experts from Vietnam to do so.

There was another bitter irony here. As the kiln devoured the sapele, it spewed into the air carbon dioxide, one of the main gases causing global warming, which an intact Congo forest helps slow. Yet in the context created by that logging operation, using the majority of the wood provided by an ancient tree as kindling and charcoal was deemed both efficient and accepted practice. How much of the Congo forest would, I wondered, become charcoal and ashes?

As the remains of the once living, vibrant tree were being turned into burnt, dead matter, the smoke, combined with the red glare of embers in the kiln, seemed to me a more-than-adequate definition of hell—and not just because smoke, soot, and red flame are the standard motifs the Christian tradition has assigned to it. It was hell because of the environmental destruction, poverty, and desperate scrambling around for resources that goes along with the burning of charcoal. It was hell because of the dehumanization that occurs when people search for riches in the mud and disease of pits and mines and mercury-tainted rivers. It was hell because the burning of wood for charcoal is a method for acquiring energy that only increases the chances of more desperation and degradation later on as wood becomes scarcer, the climate dries out, desertification intensifies, and the atmosphere and water sources are polluted or desiccated, and eventually disappear.

It is worth noting that this operation was run by a responsible company: one sensitive to the cultural and spiritual practices of the forest-dwelling Aka; concerned that when trees were cut, others weren't harmed; and committed to regenerating the forest where it had logged the trees. This was a company doing what it could to manage its section of the Congo forest sustainably.

The company was also providing jobs and income to the local people, as well as the government. It was demonstrating a commitment to a remote area of a country and region marked by political instability, massive poverty, and lack of economic opportunity. The company was also aware that timber companies from other countries were either operating in the region or waiting to take its place if it pulled out. Such companies could be less scrupulous and more destructive than this one.

When the company representative told me that millions of trees remained in the forest, he was right. The Congo forest is huge. No doubt, in time, another tree will grow in the place where the felled one once stood. But underlying our host's comment was a worldview that's all too common: that there are always more trees to be cut, more land to be utilized, more fish to be caught, more water to dam or tap, and more minerals to be mined or prospected for. It's this attitude toward the earth, that it has unlimited capacity, and the valuing of resources for what they can buy, not what they do, that has created so many of the deep ecological wounds visible across the world.

The destruction of the environment is driven by an insatiable craving for more. This desire and the capacity to forget the lessons of the past and ignore the demands of the future seem as old as time. As an episode from the Old Testament shows, God will destroy those whose appetite for more remains unquenched.

In Numbers, chapter 11, the Israelites, who have fled from Egypt into the desert, respond to a fire on the edge of their encampment by complaining to their leader, Moses, that they do not have enough food. Now, God has already miraculously supplied the Israelites with sufficient food in the form of manna. But they demand more, in particular the foods they once took for granted. "If only we had meat to eat!" they lament. "We remember the fish we used to eat in Egypt for nothing, the cucumbers, the melons, the leeks, the onions, and the garlic; but now our strength is dried up, and there is nothing at all but this manna to look at."

Moses takes the Israelites' complaint to God, who is very angry because he has provided plentiful quantities of manna in the desert. Nevertheless, he tells Moses that he will supply his people with meat, "not only [for] one day, or two days, or five days, or ten days, or twenty days, but for a whole month." There will, however, be a cost. The meat, God says, will arrive in quantity, "until it comes out of your nostrils and becomes loathsome to you—because you have rejected the Lord who is among you."

God then sends a wind that brings quails from the sea and lets them fall a day's journey from the camp. The Israelites work day and night to gather up as many quails as possible and bring them back, one trip after another: they cannot have enough and must return for *more*. However, even as they begin to eat, "while the meat was still between their teeth, before it was consumed, the anger of the Lord was kindled against the people, and the Lord struck the people with a very great plague." The writer notes that the place where the dead were buried is called "the graves of craving" (Num. 11:33).

This passage is one of many throughout the Hebrew Bible

that emphasizes the failure of the Israelites to listen to God and follow his laws. It is a story of disobedience. The fate of the quail eaters suggests that we should respect limits and not demand more than we need or can handle. After all, God has provided the Israelites with the perfect food for their situation (much as he does for Adam and Eve in the Garden of Eden), and has moreover promised them milk and honey when they arrive in the Promised Land if they obey his word.

As in many places in the Hebrew scriptures, it is made clear here that if the Israelites obey the laws of the land that God has established, the land will be fruitful; if they are disobedient and take more than God allows them, the land will produce the equivalent of thorns. Indeed, the Bible and many scriptures are replete with instructions about how to maintain the right relationship to food, the land, animals, and one another, as determined by God's word.

The word "craving," so implicated in the physical exploitation of the environment, indicates psychological desperation and spiritual weakness. It illustrates a want that goes beyond simply filling one's belly or satisfying one's thirst. I think of the Aka. The timber company in the Congo forest had tractors, trucks, boats, and chain saws that could bring down great trees in a matter of minutes, trees that had sustained the Aka in the forest, perhaps for centuries. These trees were being cut to supply timber for people far away whose tastes and desires had expanded to such an extent that they had created the capacity to infiltrate the thick forest and remove these resources. To the local people the forest was no longer a blessing but rather a curse. Their future generations would not be able to follow the streams, gather fruits and berries, hunt, and be sustained by the forests—that is, if we let them vanish.

The Source had placed the Aka in the middle of the forest, supplying them with enough knowledge and ingenuity to find roots and berries and leaves and wildlife to eat. It had provided them with the ability to domesticate a few animals, and had enabled them to bring into existence a local market where they could buy clothes. The Aka had traveled through the Congo and still the forest had stood: each tree a macrocosm with numerous ecosystems, and each tree a microcosm of the greater ecosystem around it, and then each ecosystem still further a component of the whole basin itself.

In this way, the Aka and the forest had managed to survive for centuries, perhaps thousands of years, without money or any of the pieces of furniture or commodities for which they were exchanging the natural resources. They had hunted the animals sustainably, but they were now helping to kill them in large numbers to supply the bush-meat market, which has the potential to empty the forests of wild fauna and endangered species, such as primates, that cannot be replenished.

In spite of the greater economic activity surrounding them, you could sense the *craving* among the Aka: a palpable feeling that they knew something more existed out there than what they were used to; a sense of dissatisfaction among these people that they were missing out. It was clear from their clothing and the signs of want that they were not comfortable, and were not sustaining themselves. A profound dissonance existed in the enormity of the gap between the different modes of knowledge and worldviews of the peoples concerned. It makes one wonder how it would be possible to balance such extremes with a policy that respected both the sustenance of what was left of the Aka's way of life and their environment, and the hunger the rest of the world has for what is contained in these forests. When the trees are gone, one might ask, will the cravings be satisfied? What will remain for the Aka? Indeed, what will be left of them, of who they are?

The challenge I face as the goodwill ambassador for the Congo Basin ecosystem is to straddle the divides between these different manifestations of craving: to persuade international agencies, governments, industries, peoples, and even the Aka standing on the shore to see the forest in a holistic way. The task must be to ensure that all stakeholders do not simply view the forest as a resource to be plundered but have enough compassion and respect to comprehend that not only do the Aka depend on it, so do millions of people in the countries of the entire Congo Basin, the whole of Africa, and indeed the global community.

As I write, the debate continues over how to meet the vast human needs in the countries of the Congo Basin while conserving its vast biological diversity. Development plans agreed upon by numerous countries in the region call on the governments to eradicate poverty and promise support to help them do so. But of course, many of these countries are simultaneously encouraged to exploit natural resources as a result of the insatiable demands of global trade rules, or the requirement to repay large national debts. So the exploitation of the environment continues. The paramount interest is economics and monetary value, which is why the spiritual values aren't present in the boardrooms where decisions on logging the Congo forests are made. Without these values, though, the resources are seen as something to exploit for profit, with far more value dead (as planking for a deck or hot tub or floor in developed countries) than alive, providing ecosystemic services that are, quite literally, priceless.

If these spiritual values were part of discussions about the forests, everyone, from corporations to politicians to the local communities, would look at these resources very differently. Through these values, we would develop an appreciation for the services those forests are providing not only for the Aka but as the world's "second lung," regulating the climate in Africa, China, the United States, Europe, and elsewhere. And we'd be grateful and work to protect the forests, even as we redoubled our commitment to ending the Aka's poverty.

Many people such as the Aka, who are very connected to the natural world, aren't necessarily connected by choice; close to the earth and directly reliant on its resources is where they happen to be. In the industrialized world, on the other hand, many people have become disconnected from nature. They may be equally dependent on natural resources, but the chain that connects them to the resources has many more links in it. They may have everything materially—everything the Aka don't have—but they still feel empty spiritually. They search for other forms of meaning or other ways of relating to the world. Some may visit traditional peoples like the Aka, looking for *their* truth; some will find ways that they, too, can reconnect to the earth, simply by being in nature. But sometimes those from industrialized nations don't find the answers among the indigenous peoples. For communities such as the Aka have their own ways of relating to the earth that may or may not be exportable. They may still be practicing the traditions of their ancestors, but may not be able to help explain that world to the seeker, who is trying to understand and recapture the world we *all* once lived in.

As the story in Numbers attests, the desire for more made the Israelites forget horrible experiences in Egypt such as slavery and imprisonment. At the same time, this desire itself can create intense suffering, by allowing us to disregard the past and not plan for the future. To be able to control that craving, to say, "No more, enough is enough," is a matter of monumental discipline. This will not occur unless it's linked to the raising of consciousness that is essential to healing the earth. People with this higher consciousness see the world with the right perspective. They value balance and harmony and are able to draw a line below or beyond that which they wouldn't go to to fulfill their cravings; these are among the people whose achievements we admire and whose actions inspire us.

In the industrialized regions, where people are mainly urban, overconsumption is the main craving and therefore the major ecological challenge. The wounds, though, are less visible, until one visits, for instance, a landfill or a smoggy city, or sees a polluted river with dead fish in it. In the poorer regions of the world, on the other hand, it's deprivation, due to persistent inequalities, that leads people to overexploit their local environment: to clear trees and vegetation, to cultivate crops on steep slopes or in forested areas, to induce massive soil erosion, or to overgraze their livestock and reduce pasture to near desert.

It wasn't always this way. Before the wealthy nations were as rich as they are today, thrift was a common value and older people often enjoined younger ones not to waste, whether it was fuel, food, material possessions, or their potential. The Kikuyus, for example, had many rituals and practices that expressed gratitude for the bounty of their region and its continuance. Traditionally, a small portion of the first harvest was always delivered to a specific open area or grove, away from the village and usually at a crossroad that everyone knew of. This was called the "granary of God" (*ikūmbī ria Ngai*). Here, every farmer was obliged to leave a portion of what he had harvested as a kind of tithe for the wild animals or the very poor or those who, because of a physical or mental disability, weren't able to grow or harvest their own food. In this way, the community ensured not only that there would be enough to eat, but that those less fortunate, as well as wildlife, would also have access to food. It was their way of contributing to the common good.

In a similar vein, any member of the extended family or group blessed with wealth, such as land or livestock, was obligated through custom to give the rights of cultivation to another less fortunate member of the community in genuine need of land. By providing labor to the benefactor, an individual could also earn livestock and graze them on the benefactor's land for a short time, until he could acquire his own land. Diligence and hard work were considered virtues and one did everything possible to become self-reliant and independent. Exploiting the benefactor or overextending one's stay was considered a vice, and the community exerted pressure on everyone to practice a responsible livelihood.

The Kikuyus also had a tradition of hospitality that included ensuring that no one should die of starvation while traveling through Kikuyu territory. While, of course, many travelers would have carried enough food with them to last the passage, sometimes they miscalculated the time or length of their journey, or were waylaid by bad weather or swollen rivers and thus ran short. Because of these realities, Kikuyus believed that travelers were permitted to eat food in the fields if they were hungry. Due to the fertility of the land then, the fields were full of sugarcane, sweet potatoes, and bananas (which, if not ripe, could be roasted to become edible). Significantly, however, one was only allowed to eat as much as one needed. Travelers could not carry the supply with them; that would be considered greedy and a sign of ingratitude. This custom had many impacts. First, it ensured that no one individual's land was denuded of crops, because there was a limit on how much a traveler could eat in a given period of time. And second, the remnants of the food not consumed by the traveler could be eaten by someone else or used to feed domestic or even wild animals. These two direct purposes encapsulated a third, more indirect, cultural message—that no one should be too greedy or take advantage of another's generosity. This sense of restraint was also considered a virtue.

What was taken from the fields was only what was needed and not what was desired. Waste was reduced, and as light as possible an ecological footprint was left on the land. It also offered the kind of food security that today so many in the poorer parts of the world lack. While self-reliance was essential (everyone who could cultivated food crops), the community embraced the value of service to travelers, of supporting others in times of need.

The Kikuyus did not have a particular spiritual reverence for animals apart, perhaps, from goats, which were sacrificed during various ceremonies. Nevertheless, they weren't ruthless in protecting their domesticated animals. The occasional loss of a goat to wild animals, or even the risk of hyenas eating the remains of the community's dead—who were either interred in shallow graves or even left unburied—was accepted as part of the cycle of life. Traditional Kikuyu houses also had an area inside where one's goats or sheep, especially the young and vulnerable, spent the night. Not only, of course, did this protect the animal from the elements and from being attacked by predators, but the animals kept the house warm and free of parasites such as the chigoe flea.

Because Kikuyus lived very close to their animals, they grew to know their idiosyncrasies and responded well to their needs. In an act that is still performed by millions of children in rural areas around the world, before I went to school as a child I would go into the field to check on my father's goats and sheep. When it came to killing their domestic animals, the Kikuyus had—like many traditional communities, and indeed Jewish and Muslim ritual slaughter—a set of social taboos that made it a weighty and consequential act. Permission to kill was sought from the Creator and the ancestors. To protect the animal from the trauma of instant death, it would first be denied air and blood to the brain before a knife touched its body.

Although these traditions were still alive during the early

part of the twentieth century, they quickly died out as Christianity took hold. The new cash economy created by the colonial authority, quickly embraced by the locals, and continued by postcolonial governments encouraged natives to plant cash crops such as coffee, tea, and corn. Traditional foods were trivialized and considered only suitable for the poor and unsophisticated. Not only did this mean that there wasn't extra food for the casual traveler, but the farmers themselves now did not have adequate, nutritious food. With the money earned from cash crops, native Africans began buying food, rather than producing it. The traditional diet that was mostly vegetarian and full of fresh greens—with many varieties of bananas, and grains such as sorghum and millet—gave way to imported food crops eaten in industrialized countries, a diet dominated by fats and sugars, salt, and processed foods. Needless to say, diseases associated with eating and living this way overtook the local communities with a vengeance.

Goat culture and traditions that inculcated respect and a sense of gratitude for animals sacrificed to sustain human life were abandoned. Whereas Kikuyus traditionally had eaten meat on special days or as a condiment, the more affluent they became the more they adopted the practice of the new arrivals in trying never to go a day without animal flesh. Today, even the tourism industry has joined in by starting the very popular "carnivore" restaurants, which originally featured wildlife meat. This development cultivated an appetite for bush meat that expanded to the locals. Indeed, the Kikuyus began to crave such a diet.

The craving for bush meat has meant an increase in

poaching, as the animals' skins, horns, and now flesh have a price tag on them. The land on which these animals used to roam free has been commercialized, fenced in, and privatized. In much the same way as traditional human communities are confined in their reservations, so wildlife is now enclosed in ever-diminishing parks and wilderness.

On a worldwide scale, the ravenous craving for more has very direct consequences on our environment. A 2006 study by the United Nations Food and Agriculture Organization, for example, found that the planet's livestock sector, responsible for the production and delivery of meat and dairy products, is also responsible for approximately 18 percent of global greenhouse gas emissions. This is more than the total for all forms of transportation combined and nearly on par with the greenhouse gas toll of deforestation and forest degradation. Intensive animal agriculture, and its massive requirements for feed for farmed animals, is also polluting air, water, and land around the globe, and destroying forests and grasslands.

The economy and the culture of many native peoples has shifted from a sense of collective responsibility for community well-being based on shared public space and the common good to an individualistic ethic that focuses on self. Whereas in the past the community could be defined by how it shared the bounty of the land with itself and visitors, now it is disorientated and disconnected from the land and the customs that physically, environmentally, and morally sustained them.

Such changes in the perspective on the natural world have been both cause and effect of the loss of self-respect and concern for the environment that has affected us. So much that was based on values has been lost.

The question of why humans insist on laying waste to that which keeps us alive is perhaps unanswerable. It is based on behaviors that may have been suitable for us when we were fewer in number and could destroy vegetation and move on with relatively limited effect on the environment, but that now pose a threat to our very existence. Nonetheless, although we may not know *why* we act this way, it's essential that we address the attitudes that lead us to such self-destruction before it's too late.

Along with a shift in consciousness, there is a need for a change in "perspective." We need to reflect more thoughtfully on our responsibilities to the planet and to one another, and provide a way forward to heal all these wounds by embracing creation in all its diversity, beauty, and wonder. To do so, we need to take another look at planet Earth.

CHAPTER THREE

Changing Perspectives

"I was just taking a glance out the window and I saw dozens of fires," Commander Eileen Collins, the first woman to lead a space shuttle mission for the United States, reported after she and her crew returned to Earth on the *Discovery* in August 2005. "The way they were burning, it looked like it wasn't a natural event. It was widespread.... One of the things I saw was the massive burning taking place in the central part of Africa."

What Collins told reporters that she'd glimpsed two hundred miles beneath the shuttle as it passed over Africa, including the Congo Basin forest region, was significant. "We saw deforestation," she said of the island of Madagascar. "The rivers and streams that normally would be a bluish-gray color are now brown from the erosion of soil flowing into the ocean." She added: "We would like to see, from the astronauts' point of view, people take good care of the earth and replace the resources that have been used."

What Collins had observed over parts of Africa was a cloud at once composed of sand from the desert, ash and smoke from the fires set by farmers practicing slash-and-burn agriculture and making charcoal, and loosened soil that had been caught up and was being blown by the wind. Indeed, the size of the cloud made the devastation it represented unmissable. "I'm not sure why they do that," she said.[1]

By "they," Commander Collins meant Africans. When I heard her say this, I felt the pain of recognition, since I've been saying the same thing to people for the last thirty years. It struck me as particularly poignant that throughout Africa so much damage was being done to the most fundamental elements that sustained life, and yet so many Africans were unaware of how what they were doing was undermining their own survival. At the same time, those of us who are aware of the deforestation, desertification, erosion of topsoil, and loss of biodiversity were either being ignored or hadn't yet found ways of persuading individuals and governments to take action on a large enough scale to reverse the ecological damage Commander Collins observed. In so doing, we would help stabilize the African and also the global climates.

The clouds of smoke that Collins had seen from far above the earth are one great mantle of sorrow hanging over the African continent, an omen of what awaits Africans in the near future unless we stop such thoughtless ecological destruction. I remembered God's reminder to Adam and Eve after the Fall — that they were made of dust and it was to dust that they would return (Gen. 3:19). By literally disappearing into the upper atmosphere or being blown out to sea, Africa's vanishing soil threatened to turn all life to ashes and dust.

Of course, when Commander Collins said, "I'm not sure why they do that," she could have asked that question not only of Africans, but of every citizen of the planet. For her question applies to all of us: *Why do we do this? And,* I would add, *for how long are we going to continue?*

. . .

Before we can examine these questions, we need to shift our perspective. In the late 1960s, astronauts sent back the first photographs of Earth from space and revealed to us a beautiful blue orb seemingly suspended in an endless darkness. Since then, a flood of similarly breathtaking images of our solar system and beyond has provided us with a glimpse of the astonishing vastness of the cosmos—the seemingly innumerable stars and planets, moons and comets, suns, nebulae, auroras, galaxies, and other combinations of matter and gasses. It also has confirmed that as of yet, ours appears to be the only planet where life thrives.

Not surprisingly, given the opportunity to step out of the confines of the planet's atmosphere and view the earth as a whole with their own eyes, some of the astronauts—trained as scientists and technicians, and necessarily practical and hardheaded given the danger and difficulty of their mission— either found their spiritual consciousness awakened or had their prior religious convictions deepened. In the enormity of space, despite the state-of-the-art technology and engineering they were handling, as well as the highly developed and sophisticated instruments they were employing—not to mention the calculations of astrophysicists, computer specialists, and other scientists they were drawing upon—these astronauts such as Commander Collins found themselves deeply humbled by what they saw when they looked out their windows. In their wonder, they remind us that one can be committed to the scientific method and still experience ecstasy at the great mystery of the cosmos.

James Irwin, the eighth person to walk on the moon and

who later became a minister, wrote of his view of Earth: "That beautiful, warm, living object looked so fragile, so delicate, that if you touched it with a finger it would crumble and fall apart. Seeing this has to change a man, has to make a man appreciate the creation of God and the love of God." Edgar Mitchell, the sixth man on the moon and subsequent founder of the Institute of Noetic Sciences, said: "My view of our planet was a glimpse of divinity." He added: "We went to the moon as technicians; we returned as humanitarians."

The Bulgarian cosmonaut Aleksandr Aleksandrov was similarly moved, stating: "We are all Earth's children, and we should treat her as our Mother." Sigmund Jähn, the German cosmonaut who flew on board *Soyuz 31*, said this: "Before I flew I was already aware of how small and vulnerable our planet is; but only when I saw it from space, in all its ineffable beauty and fragility, did I realize that humankind's most urgent task is to cherish and preserve it for future generations."[2]

Some of the few who saw Earth from space also wondered that life — in all its extraordinary, almost profligate variety, and protected and sustained only by the thin blue veil of the atmosphere — should have found a home on this particular planet, and that we should have emerged to be at once a part of it and observers of its existence.

Of course, you don't have to leave the planet to wonder at the unfolding universe. The two rover vehicles Spirit and Opportunity recently explored the surface of Mars; the Kepler mission searches for planets the same size as Earth; the newly repaired Hubble telescope continues to scan the farthest reaches of the universe; and the Cassini probe has beamed back extraordinarily detailed pictures of Jupiter, as well as the rings of Saturn and its many moons. With worlds upon worlds unveiling themselves to us, it is hardly surprising that our response continues to be one of awe at the complexity, beauty, and force of creation.

As Commander Collins's and other astronauts' statements reflect, when we see things from far enough away, the entire system makes itself evident to us. Such a perspective can open up deeper inquiries as to our relationship to the planet, and force us to ask questions about our attitude toward it and activities upon it—questions that, in the rush of our day-to-day lives (where we do not see our effect on the whole), we may not be able to grasp the significance of.

A change of perspective doesn't have to occur in outer space, either. When viewed from the ground, clouds can look firm and solid. But when I'm in a plane and we cut through the clouds, I'm reminded that they're just vapor. They can't hold us. Flying also offers me the opportunity to see the earth from above, and from that vantage point I'm often reminded of its fragility. As planes near Nairobi, for example, they approach the airport over Nairobi National Park, which is very close to the heart of the city. From the sky, I could chart how over the years the number of wild animals in the park has receded, and the land and habitat have been degraded. I see livestock illegally brought into the park in search of pasture when the rains fail. Beyond the park, I can see circles where the grass has dried out and areas that are in danger of becoming patches of desert.

On my trip to see the logging operation in the Republic of the Congo, as I flew over the great expanse of trees below me (and traveled up the rivers with the dense forest mantle on either side), I was simultaneously in awe at the sheer size of the area that needed to be protected and monitored, and deeply aware of how vulnerable those habitats were, and how unable the forest was to speak for itself. Like Eileen Collins, I could see from the plane's windows clouds of smoke from fires flaring from the canopy, while logging roads crisscrossed the green forest like brown scars. Being in the air helps me see the challenges the earth faces—the big picture—in a way I can't always do when I'm on the ground.

Another perspective that we all too often forget, because for most of human history it has, like the view from space, not been available to us, is the long view over time. The same telescopes and other instruments that scientists are using to observe celestial bodies and scout out potential planets that may be habitable are also now beginning to receive light from the farthest reaches of the universe, and are thus providing us with a glimpse back to its origins.

As hard as it is to grasp both intellectually and, perhaps more significantly, imaginatively the concept of the earth as one self-sustaining organism (as James Lovelock's Gaia hypothesis suggests), so is it almost beyond human capacity to conceive of space and time in this way. On the one hand, we have to comprehend the theory that at the very beginning of creation, the entire universe and all four dimensions were contained within a mass of infinite density. And that at some point beyond space and time it exploded in a set of chemical reactions that occurred within almost infinitesimally minuscule fractions of a second: the so-called big bang.

On the other hand, we are presented with the equally astonishing calculation that the cosmos has been in existence—and has continued to expand—for roughly fourteen billion years, until it is now, by some estimates, 156 billion light-years across. On top of these already boggling numbers, string theory posits perhaps multiple parallel dimensions of space and time, amid the perhaps millions of galaxies and billions of solar systems, stars, and planets.

Even when we come, literally, down to Earth—which current scientific approximations suggest emerged some four billion years ago—we are presented with eons that extend beyond our feel for the passing of time. Consider the periods of the Mesozoic era labeled the Jurassic and Cretaceous, known to most of us as the time of the dinosaurs. The word "dinosaur" is often used to describe something antiquated and obsolescent and thus a failure. Yet the Jurassic and Cretaceous periods are estimated to have extended over some 130 million years—only brought to an end by a catastrophic event that blotted out the sun and saw the planet cool so rapidly that incalculable numbers of species of plants and animals died out. From those creatures that did survive, hominids emerged only fifteen million years ago, followed by the earliest humans some eleven million years after that. The bones discovered by Louis and Mary Leakey in Olduvai Gorge in modern-day Tanzania had been in existence only for the last two hundred thousand years, while human settlements can only be dated from the invention of farming, around ten thousand years before the common era.

I recognize the value of gathering data, seeking to apply organizing principles and theories in order to understand that data, and then testing the results empirically. However, the long views that modern scientific instruments and the disciplines of archaeology and paleontology have provided glimpses of, through the vertical perspective of space or the horizontal perspective of time, offer only more wonder and astonishment: at the magnitude of created existence, and the awesome responsibility we humans have in not only comprehending it, but protecting what we can.

The world's sacred scriptures have attempted to understand this majesty through their myths of origin and their philosophies. However, awareness of these different axes of time is not confined only to the scientists or astronauts, or to those cultures that wrote their stories down. The elders, the wisdom keepers, or those who continue the traditions of their peoples over many centuries have also been able to provide knowledge of the big picture and the long view. Indeed, in the rush of scientific materialism that has swept so much of what we originally "knew" about the environment and our place within it, we may have forgotten the original majesty and awe in which that natural world was held and the ways our ancestors lived within it. The costs of the loss of this perspective are, however, all too clear.

When I visit many parts of Kenya, for example, I see a land that has been abused and the soil degraded. Few indigenous trees or crops remain; instead, nonnative plants dominate, and cash crops such as tea and coffee bushes stretch up and down hills and mountainsides. To the younger generation, however, the hillsides are lush and green precisely because of the coffee and tea bushes. They are resigned to the fact that the rivers lack water, because for them this is how the rivers have been for as long as they can remember. For the generations after this one, as the climate becomes dryer and warmer and the glaciers on Mount Kenya and the snows on Mount Kilimanjaro vanish, it will be the norm for savannahs to take the place of forests, scrub to be where once there might have been grasslands, or desert where there used to be scrub.

Kenya has been hit by recurring droughts in recent years, likely due to global warming, as well as the loss of forests and vegetation. Rivers dry up, crops fail, livestock and wildlife die, hydropower systems stop, people go hungry, and some even die. At the time of the crisis there's energy to do something to avoid another devastating drought in the future. However, as soon as the rains fall, it is as if the drought never occurred. We're like the warthog, which when it finds itself in danger— pursued by a wild dog—runs very fast. But as soon as it sees that the dog has given up the chase, the warthog stops its effort and goes back to eating as if nothing has happened, as if the wild dog would never chase it again. It forgets that the dog may have simply changed direction and be approaching from another side. The warthog quickly forgets the experience it's just had, much to its disadvantage.

Likewise, we react only to crises, not their causes, and are easily lulled into a false complacency. Many people in Kenya, for instance, have seen aerial photographs of the desiccated and barren parts of the country, and cannot believe they share the same flag. Yet what has occurred in these arid wastelands for several hundred years is what is happening to their own land. They have eyes, but they do not seem to see it.

The effects of such blindness are immediate, and can be deadly. For the last few years, Chad and Sudan have been engaged in a conflict over land. As they are fighting, the Sahara is taking over the very soil they covet. I visited Chad during the rainy season, and even though there was flooding everywhere, fields remained parched and the crops were failing. Rain is precious in this semiarid region, as it is across Africa, but I saw hardly any efforts to harvest rainwater or create terraces in fields to stop soil erosion. Now, wisdom would say, "Stop fighting. Direct all your resources that you have collectively to combat the processes of desertification: rehabilitate the land and reclaim it from a greater and unseen enemy." And yet, because of the narrowness of perspective, the leaders and people continue to fight and destroy the little they have.

Similarly, in the region of Turkana in the northernmost part of Kenya, along the border with Sudan, Uganda, and Ethiopia, droughts are now distressingly common.[3] Here it's the sense of their own powerlessness that leads many of the local Turkana and Samburu pastoralists to ascribe the drought, the consequent deaths of domestic animals, and their own hunger and thirst to an act of God. But it's a different perspective altogether that's necessary: a greater consciousness and comprehension that their circumstances are due, in part, to their own acts. When the drought first arrived, the Kenyan press reported that people in Turkana had been "reduced" to eating wild fruits and livestock carcasses in order to sustain themselves. I thought that the fact that local wild fruits had survived the drought was an excellent illustration of why we should protect local biodiversity: everything else had dried up but these wild fruits remained. The Turkana and Samburu should have planted or nurtured these species of trees that supplied the fruits and were producing something edible even in such dry conditions. The fruit from the trees reminded me of God's provision of manna—a food suited to the harsh conditions—to the Israelites in their desert.

As much as we need to take the longer view and broader perspective in seeing the whole picture, and thus arrive at sound solutions and solid practices for the changes that we must make, it's also fundamental that we pay attention to the small. Every day, it seems, we continue to gain more insight into the startling world of the atomic and subatomic building blocks of matter. While it's true that huge ice sheets breaking off from the Arctic shelf and the struggles of polar bears to hunt for seals and fish amid the shrinking ice floes provide graphic illustrations of the warming of the planet's temperatures, equally shocking are deformities in and the disappearance of smaller animals, such as amphibians, which may be caused by the increased spread and virulence of diseases, habitat destruction, and inhospitable temperatures in which to breed.

According to one scientist, perhaps as many as a third of the six thousand-plus species of frogs are threatened with extinction.[4] Creatures such as these may form a perhaps unknown link in the food chain of a particular ecosystem and the effect of whose absence may not yet be known. Dwelling on the small and its interconnectedness enables us to recognize that as much as the planet may seem to us to be a vast and complex web of ecosystems, weather patterns, ocean currents,

tectonic plate movements, and so on, it is also an infinitely subtle and intricate network of biomes that are full of microorgan-
isms, bacteria, insects, plants, and other forms of life that are
the bedrock of the larger ecosystems on which birds, bats, and
bigger, more consumptive species such as our own depend.

The Bible understands the importance of recognizing the
smallest. Jesus asks his disciples to consider the simplicity
and beauty of the lilies of the field (Matt. 6:28) and notes that
God cares for sparrows (Matt. 10:29). In the Hebrew Bible,
one of the marks of King Solomon's wisdom is his thorough
knowledge of trees—from the cedars of Lebanon to the hyssop (a shrub once used throughout the Middle East for me-
dicinal purposes), which grows in the cracks in walls (1 Kings
4:33). It is striking not only that Solomon's wisdom extends
to a discernment of the details of the natural world as well as
the human heart and its affairs, but that he recognizes that the
hyssop has its part to play in the ecosystem as much as the
cedars do.

Part of the vital need to observe the small as well as pay
attention to the large means becoming aware of the sources
of things. We don't think of those objects we use every day,
such as a telephone or a chair, as coming from a place that
could make a difference to the environment in which we live.
Even though the item in question may be small, or its impact
apparently benign, it may be part of a larger chain with much
greater consequences. The beautifully crafted chair we bought
may be made with sapele, mahogany, teak, or another tropical
hardwood, felled many thousands of miles away—a tree that
provided invaluable habitat for endangered species and whose

loss is irreplaceable because the habitat no longer supports old-growth forest. The palm oil in our soap or condiment jar may have come from a plantation that displaced the forest, the wildlife, and the forest-dwelling peoples from which the tree that provided it was harvested.

When we go to the local corner store and buy a bunch of roses to brighten up our kitchen table, we may think this is, at the least, an ecologically neutral, even aesthetically enhancing adding of color to our home. But those roses may have been flown on a jet using large amounts of fossil fuel from a flower farm in Kenya, where lake water that locals could have used to support fisheries in the lake or for drinking (or wildlife would have used for swimming or breeding in) had been diverted to grow the flowers. The potential loss of the lake would threaten wildlife and the tourism industry, on which the town also depends.

Part of acknowledging the small and its connectedness is simply in noticing individual distress and the chain reaction it could stimulate. During a recent drought in Kenya, the water level in Lake Naivasha, a center of the flower industry, dropped dramatically. One of the most disheartening consequences was that several hippos that live in the lake and graze onshore at night got stuck in the mud. They couldn't get out before they died of starvation or thirst. At the same time, water from the lake was being pumped to the flower sheds. The Green Belt Movement protested the water allocations, but to no avail. Seeing these creatures stranded and dying in the mud of the drying lake was very distressing and shook me to the core.

Of course, commerce is as essential to the developing

world as it is to industrialized countries. That is why it's important to support the fair trade movement and for us to educate ourselves as consumers on where products come from, how they are made, and the conditions for the workers who construct them. In the future, fair trade may become the typical way of doing business for whole societies rather than the niche market it mostly is today. Until then, however, by paying attention to the small, we have the opportunity to become that little bit more conscious of our decisions and be in a better position to make a positive, immediate difference.

The sacred scriptures vividly remind us of how small we are, and how embedded we must be in the ecosystems surrounding us. In the Bible, the name of the first man, Adam, is derived from *adamah*, the Hebrew word for soil. From Adam, God creates *Chava*, the Hebrew word for Eve, which means life. When I am asked about the Genesis creation story, in a light touch, I relate how God, in his infinite wisdom, waited until Friday to make human beings, and then rested on Saturday (the Sabbath). If we'd come into existence on Monday, we would have been dead by Tuesday, because there would have been nothing to sustain us!

The writer or writers of the creation story understood that we are at once the culmination of the process of creation, and yet its most dependent creature. We could *only* be created once everything else—the sun and moon, the earth and the sea and the air, and all the flora and fauna—had been separated one from the other or brought into existence. God could form humans only once there were trees to remove the carbon dioxide from the air and replace it with oxygen, and then balance the composition of the air so that the whole planet didn't burst into flame. He understood that in order for us to eat, we would need preexisting seeds. It's a sobering thought that if the human species were to become extinct, no species I know of would die out because we were not there to sustain them. Yet if some of them became extinct, human beings would also die out. That should encourage us to have respect for the other forms of life and indeed for all of creation. We should demonstrate our gratitude for the way they sustain us.

The dual position human beings have — in charge because we are most dependent, the apogee of creation because we are most vulnerable — is echoed by the apparently contradictory messages contained in both narratives of the creation of Adam and Eve (Gen. 1:26–30, 2:7–24). In the second reference, God tells Adam to serve and protect the garden; in the first, he is commanded to have dominion over the earth and subdue it. Much ink has been spilled on what the Bible means by the concept of "dominion." A consensus is emerging among theologians that the original definition of "dominion" is more accurately translated as "custodianship" or "stewardship," and that human beings do not have carte blanche to exploit nature without thinking of the consequences of our actions.

Unfortunately, it has been all too convenient for human beings to take the concept of dominion to mean absolute control over nature and exploitation without limits. Nowhere else, unfortunately, has the tragedy of this negative concept of dominion been more problematic than in the lands of many traditional communities, which came into contact with the expanding colonial world. On the one hand, they were introduced to new methods of farming, new breeds of plants that increased their yields, and machinery that made farming easier. On the other hand, however, the knowledge that had allowed them to survive in difficult circumstances was pushed aside, much as they were banished from the ownership of their own land, and their capacity for self-direction was lost. In many traditional communities, this process has led to steps both forward and backward. As the industrialized world seeks to expand its markets, it is simultaneously trying to recapture the knowledge of traditional communities, which is at risk of being "pirated," patented, and lost forever to those communities that once freely employed it.

In narrating what relationship God wishes people to have with creation, the Genesis stories make it obvious that God's primary vision, expressed in the Garden of Eden, is one of humans living in harmony with the natural world. But because of the original sin, represented by Adam and Eve's choice to eat the forbidden fruit amid the garden's bounty, they, and by extension all humans after them, are cursed. It is striking how ecological the consequences are: "Cursed is the ground because of you," says God. "In toil you shall eat of it all the days of your life; thorns and thistles it shall bring forth for you; and you shall eat the plants of the field. By the sweat of your face you shall eat bread until you return to the ground" (Gen. 3:17–18).

By placing the different concepts of dominion and protection next to each other in the Hebrew scriptures, the scribes let humans know that we have the free will to destroy or tend,

protect or subdue, act as dominators or as conservers and custodians. The consequences will be ours. Indeed, it seems to
me that the mystery of our dual identity as both the summit
and yet the most vulnerable of God's creation is literally laid
out on the page side by side, in the twin creation narratives of
Genesis 1 and 2. It is as if from the outset, the writers of the
Bible trusted the reader or listener to understand that both
were valid expressions of what it meant to be human.

When I think about the topsoil in much of Africa—so
essential to all that grows and lives—that's been denuded of
forests, trees, and shrubs and is being washed away by the
rains, I'm reminded of the etymological and theological connections to Adam and Eve, humus and life. Are we not in danger of being washed away along with the soil? Or changing the
climate so dramatically that the earth becomes inhospitable to
many life forms, including us? To echo Commander Collins:
Why would we do that?

The quest for knowledge is a fundamental part of the
human psyche: we *want* to learn how things work. It would be
hard to argue that the kind of curiosity that enabled humankind to split the atom or develop rockets was a negative trait—
even if that curiosity was ultimately exploited to create nuclear
weapons and intercontinental ballistic missiles.

As a scientist, I know it's essential that we understand as
much as we can about how biological systems function. It's
clear that we still have a great deal to learn about the earth's
extraordinarily complex set of interconnected regions. Clima-
tologists recognize that the predictive models of the effects of
global warming they are developing—while a great deal more

accurate and using more data than were available in previous years—nevertheless can speak only in terms of trends and patterns, risks and likelihoods, rather than in specificities. This is only because we still have not plumbed the depths of the astonishingly subtle and complicated weather patterns of our planet's biosphere.

We need to remind ourselves, however, that for all its extraordinary sophistication, there are many issues that modern science can't explain. By any precautionary measure, we would do well to protect some of that most elemental form of the transformation of energy from the sun into matter: photosynthesis. And as we are discovering in our exploration of space, the more data we receive, the more questions we find there are to be answered.

Nonetheless, while we may never learn or even comprehend everything there is to know about forests such as those of the Congo Basin, it seems self-evident that it would be wise not to plunder or destroy them. We may not be able to extrapolate every element of the region's biodiversity, but it seems clear that an indigenous tree provides essential services to the ecosystem in which it is located and that it would be a good idea to preserve and restore as many of such trees, and the forests they create, as we can. We may not be able to predict how severe the effects of climate change may be, but it does not seem wise to keep pumping so many greenhouse gasses into the atmosphere.

Commander Collins would probably advise that the proper, even most rational, response to the clouds of smoke, dust, and ash over Africa is not to despair of our connection to the dust from which we're made and so seek to use our technological know-how to flee to another planet. Whatever fantasies we may like to conjure of populating other galaxies or growing food and harvesting water in space, by far the simplest—as well as the closest, greatest, and most immediate—task must be to rededicate ourselves to reducing the cloud right here over our planet Earth.

If we can acknowledge hell in the charcoal pit in the middle of the Congo, so we can likewise recognize heaven in a clean, deep river full of fish and surrounded by banks lush with vegetation and wildlife; or healthy, well-nourished children eager to learn and work hard for the future; or a citizenry deeply engaged in its society and community, animated by an acknowledgment that all of the Source's handiwork is worth preserving.

Furthermore, because the dust cloud doesn't remain only over Africa—just as the rains from the Congo Basin don't just fall over the continent—what happens on one side of the planet ultimately affects everyone. If those under the cloud move because they can no longer live under it, then sooner or later they, or others like them, will end up on another's doorstep, demanding sanctuary. Neither they nor we have another planet to go to. How much easier, more secure, and more peaceful it would be to act now to make their lives more bearable than to wait until they cannot turn back.

Commander Collins's and the other astronauts' observations offer one final set of intriguing realizations: in some way we had to remove ourselves from the constraints of the world in order to see how valuable it was to us; only through the exercise of extraordinary intelligence and the expense of financial, industrial, and natural capital developed on Earth could we even contemplate establishing life on another planet; and, after all of the intensive expenditure that allows us to carry human consciousness into space, we are still left with an age-old question whose answer still eludes us: *Why do they do those things?*

The task for us in healing Earth's wounds is to find a balance between the perspectives: between the vertical and the horizontal views; the big picture and the small; between knowledge based on measurement and data and knowledge that draws on older forms of wisdom and experience. Bearing in mind these different points of view, therefore, it is time to reflect more deeply on just how we may go about employing the spiritual values that might save us, using trees as an entry point.

CHAPTER FOUR

The Power of the Tree

The first value at the center of the Green Belt Movement's work is a demonstrable love for the environment. Such a love doesn't have to be sentimental, or imply that human beings should not utilize the resources in the natural environment. Many tree seedlings and full-grown trees die because of lack of care or drought. Or they have been cut for firewood or fencing, which may have been the original purpose for which they were grown. Such use is okay, as long as the land isn't left bare, and trees and forests aren't exploited carelessly or for the gain of only a few, while many suffer the loss of the ecological services (such as regulating rainfall or stopping erosion) that the trees and forests provide.

Even before the arrival of white settlers in the early 1900s, the countryside around the five forested mountains in Kenya was intensively cultivated and relatively densely populated. Nonetheless, the native peoples maintained extensive forest reserves where populations of elephants, leopards, buffaloes, and many other animals flourished. Although trees were cut down in these reserves and elsewhere, the communities made a habit of first using underbrush and already thinned forested areas to create houses and for firewood, leaving the larger, straighter trees to stand.

Such customs allowed the local communities to practice a form of agroforestry that retained water and topsoil. Each tree that was left standing was called in Kikuyu, for example, *mūrema-kīrīti*, or "one that resists the cutting of the forest." These trees were considered the habitation of the spirits of all the trees that had been cut down. In turn, the standing trees couldn't be felled unless the spirit was transferred to another tree. This was achieved by placing a stick against the tree to be cut down and then moving it to one that was to remain standing, or by planting another tree immediately in the same place as the felled one. Clearly, such restrictions stopped wholesale deforestation from taking place.

Many communities didn't revere trees per se, but the locals did choose certain species of trees and bushes at the base of which sacrifices were performed, both for their families and for the community at large. In Kikuyuland, one of these was the *mūgumo* or fig tree (*Ficus natalensis*). Although not every fig tree was deemed worthy of veneration, Kikuyu priests performed sacrifices only where fig trees stood. Once a ceremony had been carried on around it, that fig tree and its location became sacred. My mother told me very clearly when I was a child that I was never to collect twigs for firewood from around the fig tree near our homestead since, she said, it was "a tree of God" (*mūtī wa Ngai*).

Conceiving of the fig tree as *mūtī wa Ngai* had a kind of protoecological reasoning behind it. The tree's deep root system prevented landslides and allowed rainwater to travel from underground reservoirs to the surface in the streams and rivulets that then burst through the soil. Killing or harming every fig tree would, therefore, mean destabilizing the soil and making both the conservation of water and removing it from the ground more difficult. This logic was clearly how many peoples, who may have also used their trees as sources of medicine and food, survived in environments that were sometimes harsh.

For my mother, and the generations before her, the honoring of certain trees was part of a general reverence for nature. In the Kikuyu tradition, one was obliged to remove one's sandals if you approached a tree during a ceremony or were climbing Mount Kenya, which at the turn of the last century was completely covered with trees. Even those elders with spiritual authority would walk barefoot if they went up the mountain; indeed, so sacred was the mountain that it was impermissible to even crush wild mushrooms underfoot on one's journey through its forest.

Since the beginnings of human culture, the tree has been not only a source of food, medicine, and building material but a place of healing, consolation, and connection—with other human beings and with the divine. Trees are among the oldest, as well as largest, living organisms on the planet, so it's not surprising that human beings should have conceived of them in religious terms.[1] The Jewish mystical tradition kabbalah depicts the connection between heaven and earth as an upside-down tree. The ancient Hindu texts known as the Upanishads mention the pipal (or *aśvattha*) tree, which, with its roots in heaven and its canopy in the earth, is considered to be the manifestation of Brahma in the universe. In Norse

mythology, the ash tree Yggdrasil is rooted in the underground
and its branches support the home of the gods. Indeed, in my
more fanciful moments I conceive of the tree as an upside-down
person, with her head in the soil and her legs and feet in the air.
The tree uses it roots to eat and its leaves to breathe, while the
trunk resembles the human body.

Through the symbol of the *axis mundi*—the cosmic pole
around which everything is ordered—the tree has even em-
bodied the universe itself. Ancient Egyptians believed that a
great sycamore connected the worlds of life and death and
that a huge tree arched over the earth and contained the sky
beneath it. In a story echoed in Genesis, the ancient Babylo-
nians conceived of two trees that guarded the eastern entry to
heaven. For the peoples of northern Ghana, the baobab was
the pathway by which human beings came down to earth from
heaven. The Mayan civilization of Central America venerated
the ceiba, which they called Yaxche, the Tree of Life; it supported the heavens. In its cosmology, the Zoroastrian tradition
of Persia features the Saena, or the Tree of All Healing.

Certain species of trees have also been important spiritual centers. In southern Ghana, many communities continue
to recognize as sacred the *Okoubaka aubrevillei, Milicia excelsa,*
and a species of liana, while the Shona of Zimbabwe hold that
ancestral spirits dwelled in the *mobola* plum tree. In areas of
South Africa the *marula* is considered sacred. The Yoruba of
West Africa believe that the iroko, cotton, baobab, and African
sandalwood trees are the residences of a number of deities.
Sacred groves exist in Nkoranza, Ghana, and throughout Ma-
lawi, while the grove dedicated to the *oshun,* or female god-
desses, of the Yoruba near the town of Oshogbo in Nigeria is

so important that the United Nations Educational, Scientific and Cultural Organization (UNESCO) has named it a World Heritage site. The Ndembu of Zambia, Congo, and Angola use the *muдyi* or milk tree for a number of cultural and sacred practices, as they do the *muyoomb* and *kapwiip,* which they call "the elder of all trees." Plants can be venerated even in those areas of Africa where there is less forest cover. For instance, the Tuareg of North Africa deem the *Maerua crassifolia* to be a place where spirits dwell.

The Hebrew scriptures similarly place an emphasis on trees—and not merely within the Garden of Eden—as a token of God's presence. After the flood, the dove returns with a leaf from an olive tree in its beak as a sign that Noah's ark can come to rest. The Israelite leader Joshua is believed to have established a pillar under an oak tree at which to honor Yahweh, and Abraham places his tents within sacred groves of trees in Shechem, Hebron, and Beersheba in order to be closer to God. The prophet Ezekiel conceives of God as a tree that produces water from its roots, while both Jeremiah and Hosea compare Israel to a tree. When the Israelites are forced into exile in Babylon, they famously hang their harps upon the willows, which thereafter became a symbol of mourning. In Asia, legend has it that the Buddha was born beneath a sal tree, and experienced his first deep meditative state under a rose apple before finding enlightenment underneath the bo or banyan, which thenceforth became known as the bodhi tree. In Japan, the oldest Shinto shrines are often to be found on hillsides or within groves of trees, and a religious frame of mind is one of the qualities that cultivating bonsai trees is intended to generate.

The ancient Germans considered the oak and spruce

trees to be sacred, while the ancient Greeks dedicated the laurel, olive, myrtle, ivy, and oak to Apollo, and the cypress to Hades. An oak formed the site of worship to Zeus at Dodona in Epirus, while the Romans linked the myrtle with Venus and Neptune. Plato's academy was situated in a grove of trees dedicated to Athena, the goddess of wisdom. Even today, the ancient Greek tradition of associating the olive branch with peace and the laurel wreath with achievement in competitive sports continues.

Pre-Christian Celtic lore also honored sacred forests. Some churches and cathedrals in Europe are decorated with the visage of the pre-Christian "Green Man," who was emblematic of spring and fertility, and often decorated with leaves. Within the Christian tradition, some trees play an important symbolic role. Palm leaves are strewn before Jesus as he enters Jerusalem, and the palm, cypress, myrtle, and olive all symbolize aspects of the Virgin Mary. The columns of Egyptian temples were shaped to reflect the stems of the lotus, palm, and papyrus trees, and Vitruvius, the first-century B.C.E. Roman writer on architecture, suggested that the columns of Greek and Roman temples may themselves have been modeled on tree trunks. In all such places of worship, including Christian churches and cathedrals, the areas within the buildings' colonnades mimic the cool enclosure of an opening surrounded by tall trees, whose canopy provides protection from the elements and yet whose vaulting space gives a feeling of openness and uplift that encourages a sense of the divine.

In addition to the sacred grove—a space in the forest where the divine might be experienced—many religious traditions honor the individual retiring into more intimate or stark landscapes to receive divine messages. The undulating landscape of the Central Highlands of Kenya provided many places for Kikuyu priests to escape and commune with God or to receive inspiration. Kikuyu lore has it that the Kikuyu traditions and language, which is rich with sayings and idioms, and through which efforts were made to create a form of writing, were developed between harvests in the many caves in the region by *aini a gĩchandĩ* ("players of the *gĩchandĩ*," an instrument made from a gourd). These grottos might be near waterfalls or rivers; they would be naturally covered by vegetation and thus it would be easy to secrete oneself away.

The Archangel Gabriel is thought to have given the Prophet Muhammad the Qur'an in a cave. The Hebrew prophet Elijah flees into the countryside, and hides near a brook where he is fed by ravens. The Mormon religion began when Joseph Smith received his revelations in a sacred grove in Palmyra, New York. John the Baptist, of course, prophesies the coming of the Messiah in the wilderness, and Jesus goes into the desert in order to be tested. Through the course of the three years of his ministry, Jesus retreats several times to be alone (for instance, Luke 6:12). On the last night of his freedom, he removes himself to pray in the Garden of Gethsemane. Even cathedrals and churches—which encourage such lofty senses of the divine—provide chapels where one can be alone with one's thoughts and one's God.

Because of their spiritual resonance, as well as the shade and space they offer, trees provide natural focal points for a community to come together to deliberate its future or for

elders to render judgments on contentious issues. Consequently, it's not surprising that certain trees became symbols
of a group's identity. I encountered this firsthand in 2006 in the
Basque region of northern Spain, where the local government
was partnering with the Green Belt Movement to plant trees
and offset greenhouse gas emissions. Representatives of the
administration took me to see an oak tree that marked the site
of the original Basque government. The oak, which was about
twenty years old, was said to be the fourth tree that had been
planted on that site since the fourteenth century.

The Basque people are not alone in considering a tree the
locus of judgment and government. In Kenya, Samburu leaders traditionally gather under a tree to discuss issues. The early
Israelite judge Deborah takes her seat under the palm tree to
exercise her wisdom. The Oromo of Ethiopia and Kenya deem
the scepter tree (also known as the *bokku*) a suitable place for
officials of the traditional courts to gather. The judges from
the Maasai and Kalenjin communities traditionally sat under
a tree, and once ensconced beneath it one was obliged to tell
the truth—much as placing one's hand on the Bible is meant
to encourage honesty in a court of law today. In addition to
providing shade for learning and government in Southeast
Asia, and Java in particular, the banyan has also been used
as a place under which to conduct business in Gujarat, India.[2]
The early Buddhist *sanghas* likewise practiced their austerities
within the forest.

Among Kikuyus, once men had finished raising their children, they were expected to become guardians of wisdom and
protectors of the community's way of life. As such, they were

considered peacemakers and judges, and during the ceremony inducting them into elderhood they were given a staff from the *thüigï* tree. This mark of authority allowed them to officiate in the various ceremonies and rituals that marked the communities' rites of passage and sacrifices.

When he was about to perform a ceremony, a Kikuyu elder would disappear to a special, sacred location in the forest for seven days to purify himself. The number seven signified a bad omen for Kikuyus, so staying in the forest for a week meant that the omen could be reversed. During this time, the elder would take no alcohol, and refrain from sexual activity and other pleasures. He would try to rid himself of bad thoughts and focus on the ceremony at hand: why it needed to be performed and the meaning of its practice. The ceremonies themselves were attempts to appease God, who would have precipitated whatever the community was facing: a drought, a famine, barrenness, or an epidemic of disease.

Whenever a judgment was to be made, the thiigï stick had to be present; it was the signal that violence was unacceptable. I recall my mother telling me that if there was a dispute between men from different mountain ridges, the elders from the opposing groups would meet. If they decided there was to be no conflict, rather than announcing their judgment directly to the young fighters, the elders would stand on their side of the riverbank and stretch their thiigï staffs so that they pointed toward one another. The elders would then declare a truce by saying in unison, *mbaara horoho,* or "let the conflict end." Once the elders uttered those words, the warriors would depart without speaking or showing any aggression to the other side. This ritual was as binding as a signed peace treaty, and it served very well to maintain peace within and between the communities.

It needs to be reiterated that honoring and sacramentalizing trees in these communities didn't mean that they could never be cut down or utilized for ordinary purposes. In fact, they always have been, even to make sacred spaces. The temple built by Solomon is made from oak, palm, date, and willow trees, among other natural elements. Hindu temples are often constructed of wood from the deodar.

Within the broader perspective of public policy, therefore, if trees have been grown only for timber, then it seems reasonable to cut them in their prime and use the wood. What needs to be borne in mind, however, is that the conventional economics of natural-resource use—that a tree is only as valuable as the amount of money that can be obtained for the products that can be made from it—fail to account for the many other values that human beings draw from the world around them. In fact, scientists are only now beginning to understand the vast range of services—natural, social, psychological, ecological, and economic—that forests perform: the water they clean and retain; the climate patterns they regulate; the medicines they contain; the food they supply; the soil they enrich; the carbon they entrap; the oxygen they emit; the species of flora and fauna they conserve; and the peoples whose very physical existence depends on them.

In 1997, a coalition of scientists estimated that the total dollar value of the planet's ecosystemic services was $33 trillion—or almost double the then gross national product of the United States ($18 trillion).[3] On a local level, these services can be of crucial significance. For instance, planting and ensuring the survival of 30,000 acres (12,000 hectares) of mangrove trees in Vietnam cost $1 million, but saved $7 million a year in maintenance costs for the country's dykes, according to a recent report from the United Nations Environment Programme. While shrimp farms, which often require clearing coastal mangroves, can generate (with subsidies) up to $1,220 a hectare (2.5 acres), the losses to local communities of wood and nonwood forest products, fishing, and coastal protection adds up to nearly ten times that: $12,000 a hectare. And after five years of commercial shrimp farming, when the environment is exhausted and the operations move on, restoration costs are estimated at $9,000 a hectare.[4]

That some rare tropical hardwoods are made into such functional items as boardwalks, benches, or even chopsticks — and that so much goes to waste — suggests just how far removed we are from understanding the power and value of trees and forests, and of loving the environment.

When we reflect on the sacred groves and the spiritual and symbolic weight we have given to trees and forests, it seems self-evident that not only have trees been our constant companions, but we would quite literally not be human if we didn't perhaps feel regret when a tree disappears from the landscape. For when it does, a fundamental concept from the Garden of Eden also disappears.

It is possible to live within a forest and not really *see* it, or dwell in the countryside and not appreciate and be inspired by the nature that surrounds you. The prophet Jeremiah laments those "who have eyes, but do not see, who have ears, but do not hear" (Jer. 5:21). When I raise the issue of the loss of the natural world in the Green Belt Movement's civic and environmental seminars, many participants tell me that it's as if they had looked at the world around them for the first time. "Until I took this course," one representative woman said, "I didn't see the bare fields and roadsides or the denuded landscapes. Now I see areas where there should be trees, and rivers filled with silt that I hadn't noticed before." She finally *saw* what had been in front of her all along; her consciousness had been raised, and now she was in a position to participate in the process of healing.

Perhaps this is why, as I watched that two-hundred-year-old sapele fall to the ground that day in the Congo, it felt to me as though something extraordinarily weighty and consequential had been brought low. In its collapse was an echo of the trees and whole forests disappearing all over the world. Perhaps, too, given the age of the tree, I'd recognized something of myself in it: in the passage of our many years, we had turned from limber youth to creaking old age, our fresh limbs knotted and worn by time, yet still, I hope, with a contribution to make and still holding on to our lives with an element of dignity and resilience.

I could imagine how far that tree had come, from its beginnings as a tiny seed one could hold in one's hand to a mighty organism that had outlived many generations of humans. Such a journey—nurtured in the darkness of the soil, the lightness of the sun, and the dampness of water—could be explained by science, but somehow it was still miraculous: that life of such grandeur and permanence could have emerged from something so small and fragile. The spread of the roots downward and the branches upward provided a glimpse of the beauty and complexity of natural processes that our scientific instruments, for all their sophistication, still aren't quite able to explicate.

That more than half of the wood from the tree would go up in smoke—even though it had until the moment it was cut down possessed a hardiness that enabled it to withstand storms, soak up the rain, and hold fast during dry spells—also upset me. Its branches had hosted insects of various sorts, and, despite the risk of loss of a limb or two, and the parasites and birds that may have bored holes into its trunk or eaten out its inside, it had continued to grow. But now the tree was no more because it had been judged to have greater value dead than alive.

One aspect of a love of nature that we need to foster is experiential. Nature—and in particular, the wild—feeds our spirit, and a direct encounter with it is vital in helping us appreciate and care for it. For unless we see it, smell it, or touch it, we tend to forget it, and our souls wither. This is particularly true in urban settings or industrialized countries where direct experience of the untamed is less common, and it's the main reason so many tourists visit Kenya (for the most part, they're not coming to see the Kenyan people!). They want to see the large animals in their natural habitat. Many develop a connection to a lion or an elephant or a wildebeest, and they want to help keep them alive.

In many ways, this search for the wild is an attempt to heal the "dis-ease" we all live with, since none of us is immune to the effects of environmental degradation or diminishment of the natural world. I feel it when I'm in the countryside in Kenya and see bare hillsides and rivers red with silt, which harms both people and other species. Likewise, I feel ease when I visit places where trees, particularly those planted by Green Belt Movement groups, have grown and cover a swath of green land that was once bare.

I remember on one occasion we visited a site that had been used for cash crops and then, when the soil was exhausted, abandoned. Through our efforts, the grasses and small bushes that formed the undergrowth out of which native trees could grow had returned, and vegetation covered the ground so completely that one would have been forgiven for thinking that agriculture had never taken place there. Near the site, we came across two streams, which a local forester told us had sprung up since the rehabilitation of the woodland. As we descended into a deep valley, we could see the water from the streams merging with the river, which had deepened and become enlivened. Seeing the replenishment of the deforested area and the resurgent streams almost overwhelmed me. Not only was the land recovering, but we had been instrumental in creating water where none had existed for years. It seemed like a miracle from God—like Moses striking the rock and seeing water gushing forth into the desert (see Num. 20:11)!

I'm sure I'm not alone in feeling my heart stir when I see rivers cleared of silt as forests are replanted with indigenous trees, or when I meet someone who says his life was changed by the work we have done. When we experience something pleasant, such as standing in a forest listening to the birds, the insects, and the sound of the wind in the branches, we are filled with a sense of well-being. It's as if what we're searching for finally has been found.

Certainly it's important to read about the earth, and understanding its systems also helps create a connection to it, and a desire to want to do something for it. However, if you detach yourself completely from the reality of nature, you lose a little of the knowledge about what is happening to the planet. It is worth remembering that for the last fifty years, scientists working with the soil, in the forests, and in the oceans have told the rest of the world of the mounting evidence of drastic changes to the earth because of toxic pollutants, habitat loss, species extinction, depletion of the ozone layer, and changes in climate and temperature from the greenhouse effect, which we know today as global warming. They gathered data, but they did so *within* the natural environment. This is also why I believe it's so essential to have environmental education in schools that includes experiential learning, so children can touch the soil and see the worms, or tend a garden and harvest and eat what they grow. Unfortunately, if they don't have such experiences, or if they never plant a tree, they may not know what they have missed until it's too late. They may never rediscover the lost sacred groves.

CHAPTER FIVE

Sacred Groves, Sacred No More

Through the centuries, as worldviews have collided, trees, because of their resonance and power to human beings, have become, literally, totems of the clashes between different groups. Whether trees have been understood by their communities as nodal points that connect the world above with the world below, or as places where one's ancestors and/or their spirits reside, invading forces have understood that sacred groves or trees must not only be destroyed, but that such destruction is an extremely potent way to demoralize, fragment, and intimidate the local population by stripping it of both its economic and its spiritual sources and strengths.

As many fairy tales attest, the woods can inspire fear as places of transformation where the ordered world is subjected to the disorders of Nature. The forest is where Hansel and Gretel meet the witch; Snow White flees into the woods to escape her wicked stepmother; the thorns and thickets of a hundred years have to be cut through if the prince is to rescue Sleeping Beauty; and it is in the woods where Little Red Riding Hood encounters the wolf.

Of course, these ideas say more about the social identities of the various societies and cultures that hold these concepts than they do about trees per se. For many native peoples, such as the Aka of the Congo and other forest dwellers, the forests have not been fearful places that they must conquer or where they cannot go, but their entire *world*, the source for their food and medicine, clothing and shelter. To the Aka, the forest — and indeed what the world calls the "environment" — does not exist beyond or outside the human realm. In other words, nature is not something set apart, with or against which we react. It's not a place we fear as something within which we might lose our humanity or, conversely, a place where we might gain perspective and simplicity away from the corruption and treachery of the court or the city. It is, instead, something within which human beings are enfolded.

This battle for control over the meaning of the spiritual landscape is an ancient one. An example of such a conflict can be found in the Hebrew scriptures, with the struggle of the Yahwistic priests to destroy the cult of Asherah, a goddess who in her various forms the Israelites came across once they settled in Canaan, and who was worshipped extensively during the first and second millennia before the common era. The most common form of reverence — as the writers of the books of Kings, Chronicles, Isaiah, and Jeremiah note — consisted of worshippers building "for themselves high places, pillars, and sacred poles [*asherim*] on every high hill and under every green tree" (see 1 Kings 14:23; 2 Kings 17:10, et passim). Of the twenty-two references to asherim in the Hebrew Bible, most involve either the condemnation of kings or groups who set them up or the praising of those in authority who tear them down.

Scholars have traditionally called Asherah a fertility goddess, although such a designation has been questioned.[1] In the

Kikuyu tradition, women who were unable to conceive would carry dolls on their backs and visit a fig tree, where the local holy man would conduct a ceremony. In much the same way as the maypole in Europe, the totem in various Native American cultures, and the lingams and stupas of south Asian cultures, offer connections between the tree as a symbol of power and a phallic object suggesting fertility, so the asherim may have been a sign of the ever-recurring potency of the tree, which constantly renews life, year after year.

The religious and political authorities of ancient Israel clearly considered that worship of the asherim was against Yahweh's commandment and tore down the sacred sites. Following a similar approach, saints Benedict and Boniface in the sixth and seventh centuries, as well as Charlemagne in the eighth, destroyed pre-Christian groves in Europe, not only to prove that the powers contained within the trees or groves were idolatrous and therefore no match for the Christian God but to force the locals to convert to the new faith.

Such acts of sacred vandalism for religious and political purposes are not confined to the ancient past. From the moment they set foot on foreign shores, colonial forces demonized and marginalized the religious practices of those they conquered and occupied. As with the followers of Asherah, the Kikuyus were told that God could not be worshipped outdoors, in the high places or in the forests, but that he was to be found only in the building built for him, where an altar would be set up and controlled by a priest whose authority had come not from the community but from another representative who lived many miles away.

On August 4, 1914, the British burned and destroyed the houses and sacred groves that belonged to the Giriama, a community whose ancestral home was along the coast of Kenya. Their objective was to stamp out resistance to the program of taxation and recruitment to the workforce the colonial authority intended to impose. This occurred on the same day that Britain declared war on Germany, in a global conflict that would leave millions dead among the destroyed homes, mud, and shattered tree stumps of the battlefields.

Even today, communities know that destruction of sacred trees carries a potent message. In January 2002, a minister belonging to the Assemblies of God church in Laikipia district, on the northern side of Mount Kenya, gathered members of his congregation to cut down and burn a sacred fig tree. Called *oroteti,* it was where elders had prayed and made offerings during several years of drought. On many occasions, the government of Kenya has barred some members of the Kikuyu community from praying to God facing Mount Kenya, or visiting the mountain on a spiritual pilgrimage, because such practices are deemed unacceptable by the dominant form of Christianity.

Just as invading forces know that cutting down sacred groves and trees can assist in quelling a community's recalcitrance, so resistance to the imposition of different social or religious customs, or economic agendas, has sometimes taken the form of communities rallying to protect trees. One could also see such actions as demonstrating a love for the environment.

One of the best known is from the 1970s, when rural men and women in the Indian Himalayas became distressed by the destruction logging companies were causing to their forests. The Chipko movement, as the informal groups were called (from the Hindi word meaning "to embrace"), adopted the non-violent resistance techniques of *satyagraha* (or "truth-power"), as Mahatma Gandhi named it. Risking major injury, the peasants joined their hands around trees in order to stop them from being felled. The modern Chipko movement was inspired by a "chipko" incident from the eighteenth century, when three hundred people in the village of Kherjarli in northwest India died hugging *khejri* trees, seeking to protect them from loggers dispatched by the local ruler.[2]

When I first started the Green Belt Movement, I didn't know about either the modern or the historical Chipko movements, but I quickly learned about them. In 1981, their leaders participated in a United Nations' conference on new and renewable sources of energy, which took place in Kenya. Many of us, including members of the Chipko and Green Belt movements, marched together through the streets of Nairobi to advocate that planting trees was creating renewable energy and providing firewood. Almost thirty years later, the world gathered in Copenhagen, Denmark, at a United Nations climate summit, to discuss whether avoiding deforestation and the degradation of forests, thereby protecting intact forests, would be one of the solutions to global warming.

One of the supporters of the Chipko acts of resistance in the early 1970s was the physicist and social activist Vandana Shiva, whose organization Navdanya is currently fighting to save biodiversity and the livelihoods and seed stocks of Indian farmers. Also in the Chipko tradition are the many people behind Narmada Bachao Andolan, a collection of organizations that protested the building of the dam over the Narmada River in Gujarat. Echoes of the Chipko movement's inspiration continue to this day in the Appiko movement (which means "embrace" in Kannada, the major language of Karnataka state in southern India), and with women in Himachal Pradesh in the very north of India. In 2009, they tied sacred threads, or *rakhis*, which symbolize the bond between a sister and a brother, around trees slated to be engulfed if the Renuka dam was built.[3] (Such an activism based on values founded on faith inspires me. Whenever I am in the Indian subcontinent, I am very aware of the great spiritual traditions of the land—including Hinduism, Buddhism, Jainism, Sikhism, and Islam.)

Two of the Chipko movement's principal figures, Sunderlal Bahuguna and Indu Tikekar, pointed out when they accepted the Right Livelihood Award on behalf of the movement in December 1987 that what started as an economic campaign to protect the forest as "a source of employment through tree-felling and providing raw material for industries" became something more—an act of resistance based on acknowledgment that the services that the forests provide are at once economic *and* spiritual:

> The long sufferings of hill-women have guided the activists to reach new heights in their movement, when these persevering mothers of the future generations dictated that forests were their maternal homes, which provided water, food, fodder, and fuel. Both the trees and the mothers teach that to

live and also to be ready to die for the sake of others proves to be the real fountain of bliss. Thus came the famous slogan:

> *What do the forests bear?*
> *Soil, water, and pure air;*
> *Soil, water, and pure air*
> *Are the basis of life.*[4]

Another act of resistance in the Chipko spirit occurred in 1997, when a twenty-three-year-old American, Julia Butterfly Hill, climbed an ancient redwood tree she called Luna in Northern California that was about to be logged. She lived on a tiny platform in a tent within Luna's branches for more than two years—through hot weather and cold, rainstorms, snowfall, and even a hurricane—as a protest against the cutting of these majestic trees, many of which were hundreds of years old. Her tree-sit generated tremendous media interest and brought the issue of the protection of old-growth forest in California to national and international attention. Eventually, Luna and some other redwood trees were saved, and Julia came down. (She admits she didn't plan to spend two years almost two hundred feet from the ground, and, indeed, the group that was organizing the protest against the lumber company was perhaps even more surprised than she was at the length of her stay.)

I feel kinship with Julia, not only because she saw the beauty of a tree and decided to do something to protect it and express her love for the environment, but because she recognized a wrong being done and decided to try to stop it.

While Julia was in the tree, she developed a close fellow-ship with it:

> Perched above everything and peering down, I felt as if I was standing on nothing at all, even though this massive, solid tree rose underneath me. I held on with my legs and reached my hands into the heavens. My feet could feel the power of the earth coming through Luna, while my hands felt the power of the sky. It was magical. I felt perfectly balanced. I was one with Creation.[5]

During the storms to which Julia was subjected, she found herself bending and swaying along with the branches as they tossed in the wind and rain. The tree, of course, was also help-ing sustain Julia by providing her with oxygen to breathe even as she was providing it, as she breathed out, with the carbon dioxide it needed.

To some, of course, assigning a name, a spiritual dimen-sion, or distinctiveness to trees may seem absurd; something suitable for poets and primitives, perhaps, but not a rational or scientific response to the biological cycles of decay and re-generation that have neither personality nor moral compass. Indeed, it may be pointed out that the natural world, for all its symbioses and ecological harmonies, is also one of a pitiless struggle to survive, of parasites and predators, extinctions and disease. The forests are merely one natural resource among many; our only responsibility is to use them wisely.

But the beauty of Julia's gesture was that she didn't balk at the naysayers who looked at the tree and said, in effect, there are millions of other trees in forests across the world that are being logged and that it was useless to try to save one tree or the grove that surrounded it. She didn't rationalize her gesture against the likely outcome. She simply climbed the tree, and slowly, the derision her act had received from many quarters changed to a grudging admiration; the issue of clear-cutting in the Pacific Northwest was no longer ignored; and the pressure to come to an arrangement whereby Luna might be saved (an arrangement that hadn't existed before) became too much for the forces arrayed against her to resist. Julia's act demonstrated not only a positive value but how much we've lost. That sense of beauty, awe, and harmony in nature has too often given way to another vision of what we can use, exploit, and control.

This attitude has extended to all of nature. When, for example, I look back on the Kikuyu way of life that existed before colonialism, I am sure that one of the reasons the community appeared to have so much time to celebrate and enjoy the natural world was because they weren't looking at it through acquisitive, materialistic eyes. To take just one example: They didn't go to a river trying to figure out how they could privatize the water, put it in a bottle, and sell it; they relaxed and appreciated its beauty, grew arrowroots or bananas or sugarcane along its banks, and marveled at the fish that swim in it.

If we love the environment, we must identify with the tree that is cut down, and the human and other communities that are dying because their land no longer sustains them. We must express regrets for the destroyed landscapes, become angry when we hear of another species under threat from human activity or see another polluted river or a landfill. We need to honor our hunger for beauty amid the sterility of an urban environment with no parks or trees or flowers. We need to recognize the despair we may feel when a river no longer reaches the sea, or a lake's bottom is caked with cracked mud.

What if those of us who live in environments that are threatened decided that we'd only use trees that fell and died because of weather events, disease, or age? Or that we'd only use those trees that were not essential to protect water supplies or to sustain biodiversity? We might be very challenged, of course, to continue our accumulation of goods and the improvement of quality of life that we value in monetary terms. On the other hand, we may start to replenish the stocks of water, reduce the effect of global greenhouse emissions, stop soil erosion, bring back endangered species, and support a host of other life-affirming services that we have not monetized because we assume they aren't economically important — unless we can use them in commercial activities. We might also recognize that we have a host of new friends with which to commune — the trees whose lives we spared, and that breathe in symbiosis with us. We might reduce our competition with other people over access to those trees and cultivate cultures of peace with our neighbors.

This can be done. The Green Belt Movement and the Kenyan army held civic and environment education seminars, for instance, that led to an unprecedented action. The army, whose soldiers have been trained to protect our territory against an invasion by an outside enemy, recognized that unless we take care of our water, forests, and land, not only will we Kenyans be likely to fight among ourselves for access to those resources, but the country itself will be threatened with desertification. Under the leadership of the army's chief of general staff, General Jeremiah Kianga, the Kenyan army began a campaign to protect seedlings and plant trees in their barracks, as well as inside national forests. The soldiers were quick to understand that the encroaching desert under their feet is as dangerous as a foreigner wielding a weapon who claims a part of Kenya.

The spreading of the Sahara southward and the Kalahari north is not an idle concern. As trees are cut and planting stops, even the grasses eventually vanish. The animals disappear and all that is left is sand. People are then forced to migrate and move toward areas already settled by other communities. This is already happening in places such as Darfur, in Sudan, as well as in Kenya, where struggles over land and water are politicized and often characterized as age-old tribal rivalries. Why should we be surprised that in such situations, conflict becomes more likely, and we ourselves become a little coarser, harder, more easily moved to violence because we have been cut off from that which gives us life? For we are neglecting a threat not only to our national borders but to the future of civilization. While this threat doesn't carry a gun or a bomb, it is stealthy, and over the long term it promises to be just as devastating. No weapons will counteract this threat. Only a change of consciousness that includes rediscovering that love of nature that animated the minds and souls of our ancestors can. This is when sacred groves become sacred again.

CHAPTER SIX

Gratitude and Respect

Gratitude is the simple acknowledgment of the bounty with which you have been blessed, and a sense of responsibility for using it wisely. It is a value essential to the Green Belt Movement's work, and we have promoted it through a mantra that has been central to the environmental movement in industrialized nations for years: the three R's of reduce, reuse, and recycle.

Throughout my travels around the world, I've seen how different cultures understand what is valuable to them environmentally, economically, and spiritually and what is not. For instance, in my several visits to Japan and my interactions with spiritual leaders there, I've become aware of a set of practices and beliefs that embody some of the most attractive aspects of Japanese culture. They include the tea ceremony, the Zen garden, haiku, brushstrokes in art and calligraphy, origami, bonsai, *satoyama,* and *tomoiki,* to name a few. All show an attention to detail and clarity of vision, as well as an admiration for modesty, respect, discipline, and order. The Buddhist concept of tomoiki, which encapsulates the interrelationship of humans and the natural world, and satoyama, a traditional means of balancing forests and agricultural land, are part of the sense of symmetry, beauty, and coexistence with nature that is valued in the Japanese way of life.

On my first journey to Japan, I was discussing in an interview the Green Belt Movement's work, and especially our campaign to reduce the number of thin plastic bags in the environment, thereby practicing the three R's. The interviewer, Yoshinori Kando, then chief editor for the Mainichi newspapers, shared with me that the Japanese had a similar concept, known as *mottainai*. Literally translated, the word means "don't waste!" and applies not only to objects but to resources and time. It encapsulates the gratitude we ought to feel for what the earth gives us. In addition, mottainai encompasses an attitude of respect and even reverence for what one has been lucky enough to receive and the need to use it with care, without wasting. It asks us to express gratitude for what we have, without holding on to possessions as though they *are* our identity. Mottainai is imbued with a sense of regret over not having used something appropriately and is tinged with a feeling of guilt that one should have received so much.

Traditional Japanese culture seems to have put an emphasis on coexistence with, and reverence for, the natural world. As in all societies, it's one thing to have developed these concepts; it's another to honor them through the generations. Unfortunately, this wisdom is not always reflected in all of contemporary Japan's activities.

Mottainai can speak to us at different levels. Like the three R's, reducing waste and being grateful for what has been given can be practiced not only in industrialized countries, where overconsumption and waste are rampant, but in poorer regions, where environmental devastation is causing the poor to get poorer and the ecosystems on which they depend to be further degraded, some beyond repair.

Many African cities have ever-accumulating mounds of trash, of which plastic — bags, bottles, and other packaging — is a major component. Thin plastic bags that tear or are tossed aside after a single use are ubiquitous; they are an eyesore and an environmental menace. Not only does it require fossil fuels to manufacture them, but they fly into the tops of trees, clog rivers and drainage systems, and can even be found in the stomachs of domestic animals and in national parks and reserves. Jokes circulate about how these brightly colored bags have become the new national flowers of Africa.

Inspired by my experience in Japan, the Green Belt Movement launched a mottainai campaign in Kenya intensifying our efforts to convince the government to ban production of thin plastic bags as a growing number of nations across the world have done, including Rwanda, Bangladesh, China, and Oman. The Chinese government's ban may save it as many as thirty-seven million barrels a year of the oil required to manufacture the thin plastic bags.[1] Thirteen hundred tons of oil are used in China every day to produce plastic shopping bags for supermarkets alone.[2] In the United States, the city of San Francisco has prohibited plastic bags, while Whole Foods Market has ended its use of them altogether. At an individual level, many shoppers either take their own, biodegradable bags or ensure that they reuse their plastic ones.

While advocating for a ban with public officials, the GBM has also encouraged Kenyans to avoid plastic bags and use baskets made from sisal or other biodegradable or biological materials harvested sustainably to carry their purchases home from markets or shops. By doing so, not only are citizens protecting the environment, they are also revitalizing traditional industries. If Kenya exported millions of carrying baskets, called *kiondo* in Kikuyu, woven by women from sustainably harvested sisal plants, to developed countries at a fair price to replace the thin plastic bags, the industry would contribute substantially to protecting the earth's resources while supporting rural livelihoods and fair trade.

Through a partnership between the Green Belt Movement and Mainichi newspapers, the concept of mottainai has been revitalized in Japan and is being shared with others internationally. I hope that practicing gratitude and not wasting will become a popular campaign across the world and that mottainai will become a global household word and practice.

In 2005, Japan announced a ban on plastic bags. But that doesn't mean that the "don't waste" campaign has fully succeeded. Even though Japan maintains forest cover over almost 70 percent of its land, it also imports a large amount of wood and wood products, having learned from its own history what can happen to governments when deforestation strips a country of its resources. Yet, on average, no fewer than twenty-four billion pairs of wooden, single-use chopsticks are thrown away in Japan every year. Originally, chopsticks were created as a way of using wood scraps that couldn't be employed for anything else (a form of mottainai).[3] Traditionally, the Japanese carried their own reusable chopsticks, so that wherever they went they had something with which to eat. Many supporters of the mottainai campaign in Japan have revived this custom and bring their own chopsticks to restaurants.

This spirit has the potential to inspire others to practice their own form of mottainai in their daily lives. In its small way, such a shift in thinking shows that it's possible to raise the consciousness of people to understand that we all live on the same planet, and that it's unfair and unjust for any individual to care only about how his own nation and people are affected by his actions.

The Japanese are using their affluence to promote the concept of mottainai, demonstrating that one does not have to be poor to cultivate gratitude and respect, and not waste whatever resources have been bestowed on one. The revival of the concept of mottainai should also encourage those who seek to reclaim elements of their culture that some may consider outmoded or irrelevant to the modern world, yet are part of traditional wisdom. When I first learned about the concept, I also discovered that it had fallen out of favor with many modern Japanese (mottainai's origins are in Buddhist practice, while the word itself is written, interestingly, in Chinese characters). It was seen as too old-fashioned for a country with one of the world's largest and most sophisticated economies and modern cultures.

Many Japanese told me they'd shied away from using the word "mottainai" because it reflected an earlier age when many people in Japan were poor and forced to be frugal. It's worth recalling, however, that the words "frugal" and "thrifty" have their roots not in austerity or the absence of wealth, but in the bounty and richness of a harvest that is a consequence of wise and thoughtful accumulation. Reviving these aspects of frugality and thriftiness couldn't be more timely. The global financial crisis and virtually worldwide recession of recent years have forced many governments and individuals to remember that saving is as important to individual and collective well-being as are spending money and consuming.

The concept of mottainai encourages us to go deeper into the value of gratitude than simply committing ourselves not to throw things away, consume more than we need, or spend recklessly. It asks us to cultivate reverence for the resources we use, to amplify the regret we have over the waste we produce and the time we waste not doing anything about it, and to express our gratitude for what we have received. It also demands that we appreciate where things come from and what it costs the earth to have them brought to our doorsteps.

For example, shopping for clothes is one of the major habits of people in many countries. Meeting this demand provides employment in retail, textile production, fashion design, and garment manufacturing around the world. It continues the cycle of production and consumption that allows wealth to circulate. However, the working conditions for garment workers in the developing world—where men and women (and sometimes boys and girls) may toil for many hours each day, for little money and even less rest—have raised serious concerns among labor and human-rights activists. Others argue that these jobs, however harsh the conditions, are a step up the economic ladder from the poverty many of these workers face in the countryside, or even less forgiving labor (such as prostitution and/or crime) that individuals may be obliged to turn to in order to earn an income.

After some time, even the largest closets of the affluent become so overstuffed with various garments that don't fit or have gone out of style or have simply taken up all the available storage space that they're discarded. They may be recycled as cleaning rags or insulation material, or taken to charity shops. However, even charity shops in the industrialized world cannot resell all the clothes they receive, so they may take them to the landfill or send them overseas so people in the developing world can buy and wear them.

When these clothes arrive in poorer countries, they're often seen as both more fashionable and more desirable than those made locally, and are often less expensive, too. The result is that retail, textile production, fashion design, cultivation of fibers such as cotton, and clothes manufacturing in the developing world—which could employ people in the communities just as satisfactorily, if not more so, than the manufacturing "sweatshops"—are collapsing; or, if they're still functioning, they are now busy making products to ship to the industrialized world, leaving nothing for the locals to wear but imported secondhand clothing. This has happened in Kenya, with devastating consequences for the local textile industry, employment, and cotton farmers.

Obviously, it is difficult to judge what "too little" or "too much" mean for different societies. However, consider the Aka in the Republic of the Congo. If they were asked what they wanted, they would probably say food, clothing, a school for their children, or a health clinic. If they were to acquire these items, they might then ask for books, teachers, and a hospital. And after that, they might ask for bicycles so they could ride into town, and then a car so they wouldn't have to expend so much effort. All of these are reasonable requests—basic provisions that are taken for granted by many people living in the industrialized world. Indeed, those of us who have access to the benefits of education or transport or food might say that what these Congolese desire falls under the category of *needs* and not *wants*. In other words, these products or services are fundamental to the possibility of development and a better quality of life. How could one disagree? Dehumanizing poverty is also a wound that calls for healing.

However, many of the ideas we entertain about whether we have enough and are well-off are based as much on our exposure to other people's lifestyles as they are on any latent sense we may feel that our lives are inherently unsatisfactory. And it is not always the case that owning more material possessions makes one more contented with one's life—or more grateful.

Nonetheless, even those who cling to the idea that all technology and modern inventions have been detrimental cannot deny that a great deal of progress was made in the last century in assisting people to live longer and healthier lives. Smallpox and polio have been virtually eradicated; more individuals than ever before have access to the mobility and opportunities that technology can provide. Furthermore, science has made great leaps forward over the last fifty years in understanding the workings of the natural world. Therefore, we should not reject outright further analysis and utilization of natural materials because of a belief in the supposed purity of "nature."

Such a critique also extends to social advancement. In the case of the communities with which the Green Belt Movement works, it would be hard to convince anyone that living in a mud hut in the countryside offers a better life than inhabiting a stone building in the capital city of Nairobi, with electricity and running water, or that people would be more content with their lot if they were unable to read and write. I myself am a direct beneficiary of these developments, and it would be hypocritical of me if I didn't admit how important they've been in enabling me to pursue my aspirations and potential.

However, we cannot escape the enormous challenge the human community faces. Insofar as billions of people now have access to wealth, infrastructure, and the material possessions of a consumer lifestyle, many billions more want the same. And all signs indicate that we cannot provide this level of wealth and comfort *using our current means of production* without threatening the life systems upon which all wealth and civilization and other species depend.

The ironies, of course, are numerous. The very countries that from the sixteenth through the twenty-first centuries were instrumental in conquering and destroying civilizations, enslaving and undermining the self-confidence of peoples, and benefiting from the pillaging of the natural resources of other communities are those whose citizens are most informed about what is happening to the planet, and who have most wholly embraced the environmental agenda. More citizens in the developed world are practicing the three R's and mottainai. More are committing resources to developing renewable energy, and endeavoring in their workplaces, homes, and communities to shrink their large ecological footprints, while attempting to reduce the greenhouse gas emissions for which their societies have been overwhelmingly responsible.

Yet many industrialized countries, having denuded their own natural resources, are now prospecting in the developing world—a de facto admission that the extractive and wasteful model of industrial growth is unsustainable. Ironically, the areas of the world where natural resources are most abundant are politically, socially, and economically among the most unstable and impoverished. In those countries whose economies are still based on the export of primary commodities (such as timber, minerals, oil, coffee, wheat, and soy), including a number in sub-Saharan Africa, many of the world's poorest people are degrading the environment, the natural capital on which they depend, to alarming degrees.

The peoples of these regions have been told so often that they are poor and powerless that they do not recognize the abundance surrounding them. Thus they can be persuaded by unscrupulous companies in league with corrupt national and local politicians to sell what they "own" for a fraction of its actual value. Even were they to embrace a new agenda that put the earth at its center, Africans might find that they cannot reach their goals because the resources (or the technologies needed to access those resources) are not available to them. It's as if someone is being swept along in the current of the river, and you are on the riverbank telling her that if she calmed down and thought for a second, she'd be able to help herself by swimming to the bank and not drowning. But the current is strong, and getting stronger; she is panicking and fighting the current, and as a result only increasing her chances that she will drown.

Where material wealth rises—often at the expense of the immediate environment in the form of pollution, waste, and destruction of natural resources—it seems that only when people feel a basal level of comfort are they are able to examine the costs of their lifestyle. By then, however, much may have already been lost. And of course, no society has ever declared that it has enough. Part of the reason for the current environmental crisis is that we're failing to imagine a different way of being in the world or to acknowledge the global reach of what once were regional or local problems.

We all have a need to feel at ease and in harmony with ourselves and the environment within which we live. Many of us discover that it isn't material things that provide this. We find that well-being and satisfaction are achieved through compassion, the giving of oneself, serving others, and sharing. We aren't material beings; we are filled with spirit. That's why many people, even the wealthy and powerful, or royalty such as Prince Siddhartha Gautama, who ultimately became the Buddha, have abandoned their material possessions to find something more valuable: something untouchable, almost beyond reach. Christ said to the searching young man who came to seek advice on how to share in the joy of paradise: "Go, sell your possessions, and give the money to the poor, and you will have treasure in heaven; then come, follow me." The Gospel continues that the young man went away sorrowfully, "for he had many possessions" (Matt. 19:20–22). Jesus was calling him to a higher level of consciousness, but he didn't want to realize it then.

Unfortunately, it's true that the more we acquire, the more most of us get a taste for acquisition, and the more reasons we find to justify that acquisition. And it is upon this fragile sense of dissatisfaction and the relative worth of our lives that the entire edifice of consumption and production appears to be built. Mottainai—with its tint of shame at having so much and the concomitant sense of guilt at not using what one has appropriately—offers a corrective to the assumption that we can continue to say yes to everything we want, and find a way to make it possible.

So, how do we reflect mottainai personally in our everyday lives? In more affluent societies, some people walk or take public transport or even ride a bicycle instead of driving. Some use water sparingly, reduce electricity usage, and carry a basket for shopping instead of using plastic bags. Those living in industrialized countries can insulate their houses and change lightbulbs to compact fluorescents or light-emitting diodes, and buy energy-efficient household machines. They can paint the tops of their buildings white to cool cities by reflecting light and heat back into space rather than absorbing it via black-tarred roofs into houses and onto the streets.

We can all flush our toilets less often or with less water, and find ways to harvest rainwater. We can support organic production, eat locally produced foods with a small climate footprint, and consume less meat. We can all work to prevent deforestation and degradation of existing forests, stop slash-and-burn agriculture, and instead adopt practices that halt the loss of soil and biodiversity. Everyone can plant trees and shrubs, and create shade and habitat for wildlife.

There are many ordinary, easily achievable actions that can bring about meaningful change in our daily lives. Like the simple act of planting a tree, performing these tasks may not appear to amount to much at the individual level. But they are an essential part of concentrating on the small. We may not see the result of these activities from space; even our neighbors may not even notice them. But if many people took one, two, or all of these steps, the impacts could be huge.

These are only some of the practical applications of gratitude. However, in that they ask us to recognize a higher purpose beyond ourselves, the world's spiritual traditions are well placed to help us not only appreciate the possibility of limits, but foster a feeling of gratitude and respect for the earth's resources. For instance, mottainai for me calls upon the same impulses of good stewardship that God demands of Adam in the Garden of Eden. Although the human being is given permission to use the resources he finds there, he must be respectful of and grateful for them, recognizing that some are off-limits, and that he should not waste either them or the opportunity to be a good steward.

Some religions have a tradition of monasticism, whereby groups of people live within communities and discipline their bodily wants — for sex, alcohol, drugs, or other kinds of stimulation — through practices that they feel bring them closer to the Source. In the Christian Benedictine tradition, for instance, monastics take vows of poverty, obedience, and chastity. Saint Benedict (480–547) founded his order in response to what he perceived to be the excesses of his society and the laxness of the contemporary monastic orders. He offered what became known as "the Rule," a practical and spiritual guidebook for individuals in community to deepen their daily lives so they'd invest all aspects of their time on the earth with godliness.

Many monastics have found that renunciation of material possessions has not limited their enjoyment of life; to the contrary, it has freed them from worrying that someone might steal what they have or from spending so much time on technological diversion that one fails to appropriately value relationships, the natural world, or the Source. Some monastics have made a commitment to walk with the poor, not merely to help them meet their daily needs or to bear witness to their suffering, but to show to those of us not living at subsistence level that it is possible to retain one's full human dignity even without excess provisions.

Of course, like all institutions, the religious orders have not always retained either their modesty or their commitment to poverty. Some have acquired great wealth and influence through the ownership of land and have lost their moral authority because of corruption and the human failings of their members.

Apart from, perhaps, the earliest Buddhist orders, which consisted of a community or *sangha* of forest dwellers, who went into towns to beg for food in exchange for prayers being said on behalf of the giver, most monastic orders have maintained basic comforts (such as ready access to food and shelter) so they may concentrate on their work of faith. In their commitment to the poor and the sick, these orders have recognized that grinding poverty is not a righteous condition, and that willful asceticism may be as much a barrier to spiritual growth as is excessive consumption. As a result, they have attempted to formulate what Buddhists might call "a middle way," a balance between having too much and not enough.

Being grateful for what the earth has provided, and allowing ourselves and nature a chance to regenerate—both to restock and to take stock, as it were—is a concept familiar to several religious traditions. In Judaism, for instance, a special day is set aside for planting or tithing trees—Tu B'Shevat. In the Hebrew calendar, the day following the week of Creation is considered a day of rest (Shabbat), as is the seventh year. During the seventh year, the land is to be kept fallow and the food that grows naturally should be available to the poor.

Every fifty years—or seven times the seventh year, plus one—the Jubilee celebrates a redistribution of land that was unfairly or improperly acquired and a canceling of outstanding debts. This year was intended to acknowledge the inherent goodness of God's creation and to recognize that whatever had been perpetrated between an individual or a group of people may have occurred in the distant past, and even been done unintentionally, but nonetheless a wrong had been committed and it needed to be rectified. The Jubilee year provided an opening for the community as a whole to start again, to offer amnesty to the imprisoned, realign itself on the course it originally set for itself, and clean the slate of grudges that had poisoned the peoples' collective well-being and attitudes toward one another.

Zalman Schachter-Shalomi, an Austrian-born rabbi whose family fled the Holocaust and ended up in the United States, coined the term "eco-kosher" in the late 1970s as a way of modernizing Jewish dietary laws (kashrut) and practices to reflect a contemporary environmental awareness. Another U.S.-based rabbi, Arthur Waskow, has further popularized the concept of

eco-kosher, which ties ethical concerns for how food is produced (including its ecological impacts, the labor practices
used, and concern for animal welfare) with kashrut. Revivi-
fying the meaning of the Sabbath and Jubilee, caring for the
world (*bal taschit*), and treating animals humanely (*tza'ar ba'alei
chai'im*) form a coherent set of actions that honor the ancient
wisdom contained within the Hebrew scriptures with a commitment to confronting the particular environmental challenges
of today. (According to Rabbi Schachter-Shalomi, using a Sty-
rofoam cup might be suitable for someone keeping kosher, but
not for someone keeping eco-kosher.) Behind this spirit of conservation and celebration of weekly, yearly, and generational
rest and replenishment is a further dedication to the ancient
Jewish mandate to "repair the world" (*tikkun olam*).[4]

Of course, many religious traditions practice degrees of
austerity that aim to encourage a higher state of consciousness.
Hinduism values the *yamas*, or codes of conduct, which include a
commitment to nonviolence (*ahimsa*), truthfulness (*satya*), non-
stealing (*asteya*), continence (*brahmacharya*), and honesty (*ar-
java*). Many religious practices call for a blessing before meals,
while the three Abrahamic faiths include an extended period for
fasting, prayer, and reflection. Ramadan, Lent, and Passover instill not only a sense of God-consciousness in the passage of the
day, but through abstention from the satisfaction of our desires
for food, sex, and alcohol, we are encouraged to be thankful for
what we have during the rest of the year.

While the Kikuyu tradition didn't include a concept of
Sunday or an extended period of time such as Lent, ceremonies did exist that mandated an interlude of rest. For example,

the day after a burial, people didn't work (even the animals weren't allowed to go into the fields to graze—*mūthenya wa mūtiiro*). Forcing every being to stop his or her normal activities for a day served an important psychological purpose of ensuring that the bereaved recognized that life couldn't continue as if nothing had happened. It was also time to express gratitude, respect, and appreciation for the one who had left them to join the ancestors, and also perhaps to reflect on the meaning of life and death.

Rest from work also took place when communities were waiting for grain to be ready for harvest and were fending off the birds tempted by the ripening crop. During this time, young people participated in dances—celebrations that continued after the harvest, when porridge was made from the grain. The Kikuyus recognized how important it was for the community to bond through the sharing of food and, through the harvest, to acknowledge the value of collective labor and the fruits of the earth. In the same way, myriad religious and cultural traditions celebrate harvest festivals to meet the same impulse to express gratitude for bounty.

The Kikuyus were acutely aware of how essential it was to be grateful and not waste. They knew that taking abundance for granted would make them less careful, and so more at risk should fortune turn against them. If a harvest was too bounteous or livestock were producing too many calves or kids, the community would make sure that people fasted before conducting a ceremony to allow them to eat food from that harvest (to remember what it was to have little). In the case of livestock, some of the animals would be sacrificed to reduce their numbers even as people expressed gratitude to Ngai, the one who distributes the gifts." In these disparate ways, members of the community were thanking God for what they had been lucky enough to receive, practicing humility for his generosity toward them, along with feeling almost a sense of regret for the excess. In appeasing the Source, the Kikuyus prayed that they would not be punished for too much good fortune, that God would not give with one hand and take away with the other.

A similar understanding exists in the well-known story in Genesis 41 of Joseph's interpretation of Pharaoh's dream of seven fat cows and seven lean cows and seven fat cornstalks and seven thin ones. Joseph reminds Pharaoh that it is wise to save when you have plenty so you are supplied with enough when conditions are unfavorable. As a result of his wisdom, Joseph is removed from prison to become overseer of the land. We are beginning to experience challenges on a global scale to conserve water, arable land, fish stocks, and forests, while continuing to feed a growing human population with increasing demands for energy. As such, prudence, thrift, and conservation are not qualities to be practiced only in a monastic environment, or personal virtues practiced only by the righteous and pious, but are the very means of survival.

Although the Bible (for instance, Deut. 20:19–20, 22:6; Lev. 22:28; Num. 35:3–4) may offer instruction to care for the earth and not to waste God's creation, some aspects of contemporary Christian culture unfortunately encourage precisely the reverse. One song that is very popular for funerals in Kenya is "This World Is Not My Home," by the American Gospel music composer Albert E. Brumley. The song's lyrics reflect on Christians' true home being in heaven: "My treasures are laid up somewhere beyond the blue."

Some of the faithful tend to take these words literally, and ignore the bounty the Lord has given them on this planet. Even though they say they cannot be bothered with earthly things, they still need food, clean drinking water, and air to breathe. They are, therefore, not being honest with themselves. Surely, to be able to respond to a planet that is being destroyed and may soon not be able to sustain them, the faithful would help themselves if they were to sing: "This world *is definitely* my home," and "I'm *not* just passing through."

While the vision of a better world beyond this one espoused in "This World Is Not My Home" might provide comfort to those who have lost someone they love, and it may be true that heaven will be very different from earth, this song and some scriptures like it have been misused. They have created an attitude whereby people expect others, including God, to take care of them, and to fix everything that is not right about their environment and their lives.

This encourages a belief that the environment around us is really not that important. Such a worldview is directly opposed to the value of gratitude and respect for what the earth provides. After all, with such a worldview, why would it be necessary to plant a tree or protect a forest or reduce one's environmental footprint, if, as the song suggests, a better place awaits that is full of treasure and is a more suitable home? If one's *oikia*—the ancient Greek word for "home," from which we derive the prefix "eco-"—is no longer the place where one

feels one belongs and one is "just passing through," then neither *eco*logical nor *eco*nomic security are likely to matter much
in people's daily lives. Furthermore, immediate gratification
and intoxification become more attractive, because life on this
earth is seemingly worthless.

During the GBM civic and environmental education ses-
sions, many people voice their belief that heaven will be paved
with gold. Yet none of them has ever seen gold! I wonder how
one visualizes what one has never experienced. I challenge
them to think that God wishes us to care for the earth, and
that this planet might be the heaven we seek, in effect creating
heaven on earth by our own actions. I ask them: If they cannot
be trusted with what is here on earth, how will God entrust
them with what they imagine awaits them in heaven?

Sometimes, participants have their level of consciousness
raised and become willing to look at the earth as a great gift of
which we should all be taking great care. At other times, however, those who seek to justify their view that this world is not
the "real" one point to the Book of Revelation and how a cata-
clysmic event of enormous disruption will signal the end of this
world and the arrival of the Messiah. However, I don't read
the eschatological visions contained in Revelation in this way.
After all, these are not the only visions of the End Times in the
Bible: Isaiah, for instance, foresees a world of peace without
predation or want (Isa. 11:6); both Isaiah and Ezekiel envision
a destruction of all weapons (Ezek. 39:9; Isa. 2:4); and both
prophesy that God will make the land fruitful (Isa. 51:3; Ezek.
36:29–30). "The mountains shall drip sweet wine," says Amos
(9:13–15), "and all the hills shall flow with it."

Even Revelation itself describes the passing away of the "first earth" and the "new heaven and a new earth" that will takes its place (Rev. 21:1) in terms of a verdant scene:

> Then the angel showed me the river of the water of life, bright as crystal, flowing from the throne of God and of the Lamb through the middle of the street of the city. On either side of the river is the tree of life with its twelve kinds of fruit, producing its fruit each month; and the leaves of the tree are for the healing of the nations (Rev. 22:1–2).

This is what these prophets dreamed the world might become upon the arrival of the Messiah. The argument is not to reject the world we have now in the *hopeful* expectation that it will be destroyed and replaced by something better. Instead, I see them depicting an alternative to the degradation of the environment that has turned waters of life here on earth that were "bright as crystal" into mud and silt, and the "tree of life with its twelve kinds of fruit" into stumps and charcoal, and has led to nations not being healed, but rather fighting one another for access to the remaining clean water and food supplies. Like Commander Collins, these prophets are asking why we do this to the earth, and they are commanding us to heal and replenish it now.

Finally, gratitude should involve a respect for the generosity of others. Over the decades, Africa has been the recipient of considerable assistance. (The reasons many countries have made so little progress, despite the support, are corruption and mismanagement, topics addressed in great detail in my book *The Challenge for Africa*.) The Green Belt Movement, too, has benefited from the philanthropy of many friends and supporters.

What has concerned me about this external aid and support is the relationship between the giver and the recipient. Unfortunately, those on the receiving end often develop a sense of entitlement and fail completely to express gratitude for the support that philanthropists or institutional donors have provided them over the years, and that allows them to continue or expand their work. Sometimes this is the result of corruption and language barriers, which keep ordinary citizens unaware of what their leaders receive from others on their behalf. At the same time, however, those in a position to receive the aid, and who therefore understand the debt of gratitude they owe, still often demonstrate the opposite: of taking resources for granted, of undervaluing the openhandedness expressed by many individuals and institutions the world over.

These are aspects of a failure to practice mottainai and to show appreciation for those who serve for the common good. Instead, such service is taken for granted. Many countries that receive aid are comparatively young politically; many were colonies until well beyond the end of the Second World War. Regrettably, for the most part they have not adopted a culture of recognizing their citizens' service, through, for example, awards, medals, or citations, similar to those in industrialized countries. (For many, such recognition is their only reward.) To some degree, this is because those with political power often do not want to acknowledge the work of ordinary citizens.

The church partly invented the concept of sainthood to express gratitude to often wealthy or noble people who had served the poor and the sick. The designation of sainthood indicated to other faithful that these men and women were heroes and heroines to be thanked, respected, and emulated. To be sure, neither saints nor activists are immune to making mistakes. None is endowed with supernatural powers or perception. All are human beings. But we ought to reward them with some of the tenets of mottainai: gratitude and a desire to cherish and not waste the values they express in the world.

I have been fortunate to have had my work with the Green Belt Movement recognized and to have been told: "Good job." Such acknowledgment, through an award, citation, or even a kind word, can be extremely encouraging. It helps to provide the courage to continue one's work in difficult or even threatening circumstances. Even the simple act of saying thank you to someone working for the common good can reinforce, validate, and even replenish his or her energy, focus, and commitment. Because most of us tend to focus on what (or who) isn't working effectively, we may forget those who are working hard to heal the earth, and the reality that when a wound *is* healed, all of us benefit.

One physical manifestation of the kind of interpersonal gratitude that I find resonant also comes, appropriately, from Japan: that of *furoshiki*. A furoshiki is an often brightly decorated piece of cloth in which the Japanese wrap gifts. In Japan, it is traditional to present a gift when you visit someone. When your host receives the gift, she or he unwraps the furoshiki and then returns it to you for future use. When one thinks of the colossal amount of packaging and wrapping that is often tossed aside and thrown away after a present has been opened, the genius and simplicity of the furoshiki become all the more evident (according to one website, the United Kingdom generates three million tons of rubbish in the Christmas period alone).[5] After all, the social value lies in the gift itself, the thoughtfulness of the choice, and the respect shown by the giver, not in how pretty the short-lived wrapping is or how quickly one can tear it off.

Indeed, the act of giving governed by the furoshiki is more accurately considered a ritual of exchange, since the formal handing over of a gift is balanced by the receiver's returning of the wrapping. Not only can the packaging be reused and thereby the amount of waste reduced, but the giver and receiver of the gift both recognize that their friendship is not only contained between them, but it is part of a longer chain of givers and receivers, who have over time been handed the furoshiki and returned it.

The furoshiki reminds me of the Kikuyu *kĩondo*, the multipurpose basket made by women in which you would bring a gift when you came to visit, and that would be given back to you when you departed. Among the Kikuyu women, the basket would often be returned with something small inside, but not any part of what the giver had presented to the host. This demonstrated appreciation of and gratitude for being generous.

Kikuyus also used a gourd, in which they carried porridge or beer, as an offering or gift. Whoever received the gourd would polish it with castor oil before returning it. Over time, the gourd would become beautifully varnished by this repeated polishing. The deeper the color of the gourd, the more generous you had been—and the more connected you remained to the world around you. The Kikuyu saying *kanya gatune nĩ mwamũkanĩro* is an expression of gratitude for the exchange of gifts.

These gestures of giving capture both the spiritual and the practical elements of gratitude and respect for resources. Our connections to the planet *and* one another are reinforced simultaneously. The spirit of not wasting, because we assign value to something, is found in many traditions, but not often expressed. We could benefit from spending more time polishing our gourds for one another, and taking time to express our respect and gratitude.

CHAPTER SEVEN

Self-Empowerment

On a Sunday morning in November, I spoke at a church at the invitation of the local priest. As in many African churches on Sundays, the pews were full. The theme of my talk was climate change and I began with a series of questions. "How many of you," I asked the congregation, "crossed a river on your way to church this morning?" A few members raised their hands. "How many of you crossed what you'd heard was once a river, but has since dried up?" A few more hands went up. "How many of you," I continued, "drank water from a river?" Still more hands. I could tell I'd gotten their attention. They were intrigued: Where was this sermon going?

I asked how many people had eucalyptus trees on their land. A virtual forest of hands faced me. Eucalyptus is an exotic species native to Australia that the British imported to Kenya for use as timber. Although the variety introduced into Kenya grows fast, eucalyptuses nonetheless require huge amounts of water. Originally, they were used to dry marshland to make it available for agriculture. To maintain this fast growth, eucalyptuses are planted along riverbeds, in wetlands, and in forested mountains. They are responsible for the widespread desiccation of the soil wherever they've been planted throughout the country. The situation had become so serious during a recent prolonged drought that the minister of the environment had called for all eucalyptus trees in riverine areas to be removed.

As I continued, I referred the congregation to the environment minister's directive and asked: "So how many of you will dig up the eucalyptus trees on your land?" Some hands stayed raised. I explained how important it was to plant indigenous trees on their land. Such trees, while perhaps slower growing than the eucalyptus, would protect the water supply and allow the faithful to cross more (or deeper) rivers on their way to church on future Sundays. Many of the congregants nodded their agreement.

Then I asked: "How many of you are saved?" Everyone in that church raised his or her hand. "Was it Jesus who saved you?" Of course," people shouted. "And, did you know," I continued, "that Jesus died on a cross? A wooden cross?" Yes, all of them did. Now they were excited. They didn't quite know what I was going to say next. "Somebody had to go into the forest and cut down a tree and prepare it for Jesus to be crucified on," I continued. Members of the congregation were practically falling over themselves with laughter. They saw the direction my line of argument was heading. "So," I concluded, "if every one of you has been saved by Jesus Christ and is grateful for the salvation you received because of that one tree, then you should be saying thank you to every tree you see." Then I turned to the bishop and said: "That's why I'm asking the bishop to tell the faithful to plant a tree during Easter as a way to say thank you to Jesus for dying on the cross for me."

In Kenya, the annual Easter holiday lasts four days, from Good Friday through to Holy Monday. "Can't you plant one tree during those four days?" I asked the congregation. "How many of you will plant next Easter Monday?" I persisted. Everyone put up a hand. "How many of you will really do it?" I continued. People laughed. I laughed, too, as I delivered my final line: "I should be a bishop," I told them. "If I had on a purple miter, you'd take me seriously." When I finished, the bishop asked the congregation another question. "How many of you feel you have been preached to today?" And they all raised their hands.

Now, I have no way of knowing whether come March or April the following year, any of those congregants, let alone the bishop, remembered that they committed themselves to planting a tree. But at least the people in those pews on that Sunday were actively engaged in a church service and were encouraged to think about why their rivers were drying up and where the cross upon which Christ was crucified came from. My sermon was not, to be sure, theologically sophisticated; but I felt it spoke to the immediate issues that these people faced, and it provided them with a visceral connection to Jesus' sacrifice.

Even though my message may have been accompanied by laughter, I wanted the congregation to take the gesture of planting a tree during the Easter period seriously for a number of reasons. In the Northern Hemisphere, Easter is associated with the approach of spring, where the deciduous trees that have "died" through their loss of leaves in the autumn are renewed miraculously as the buds and blossoms reappear. The sun comes up earlier, the land returns to life, the sap rises, and the energy associated with rebirth and new growth is everywhere. As such, the planting of a new tree—a symbolic replacing of Christ's tree

of death with a tree that can bring life and food to many creatures (including humans)—offers a parallel both to the Christian message of life conquering death and the older traditions of
celebrating the seasonal cycle through an acknowledgment of
the transition from the darkness of winter to new life.

The planting of a tree is also a reflection of, and it is hoped
a stimulant toward, a new consciousness of the nature of the
salvation that Christ offered. To make the connection even
more explicit, Christian theology draws a link between the tree
in the Garden of Eden, cause of the Fall, and the death upon
another tree—the cross—of the second Adam, who redeems
that original sin and reverses Adam's curse. As the Gospel of
John (3:16) makes clear: "God so loved *the world* that he gave
his only Son, so that everyone who believes in him may not
perish but may have eternal life" (my italics). Our belief in
that redemption is consequential to the whole world, which,
as the psalms suggest, praise God's handiwork (Ps. 19:1) and
express abundance (Ps. 65:9–13). As the passage from John
makes clear, we have a special responsibility also in our belief,
which is to care for all the life forms we share this planet with.

Whenever I, and others within the Green Belt Movement,
use the Bible in church or during the civic and environmental
seminars, we feel it's important not to criticize or accidentally
belittle anyone's faith, which may be grounded in a completely
literal reading of the text, communicated through their priest.
We try to make sure that we speak, as I did that Sunday, in a
lighthearted manner. We also do not suggest that people see
God or the Source in elements of the natural world, lest we be
accused of pantheism.

Instead, we encourage the communities we work with to

consider the creation they read about in the Old Testament: the trees, the animals, the insects, the water, clean air, and the forests. We urge them to care for it, because the God they worship has made it, and "the earth is the Lord's and all that is in it" (Ps. 24:1). We ask them: "If you look around and if the land has been deforested or degraded, can you, too, say, as God did of his creation in Genesis, 'It is good'?" They know they cannot. In that raising of consciousness, however, the aim is not to reprimand believers for not following scripture, or for the shortsightedness of their own actions. It is to prick their conscience and provide them with serious information that we hope will make them think and spur them to action.

We also want to urge them to embrace another value at the heart of the Green Belt Movement's work: self-empowerment, or perhaps more colloquially, self-betterment. We want them to reject the passivity many display in their lives, even as they're animated by, and passionate about, their faith. We want them to embrace the belief that one *can* improve one's life and circumstances—and the earth itself. That they don't need to wait for someone else, whether of this world or another, to do it for them. That they have the capacity to provide all the energy required to heal the earth and themselves, and they cannot wait for others to do both for them. To that extent, we always encourage participants in the seminars to list their problems and see how many are of their own making and that they can solve by themselves. Through accepting their own responsibility, they can empower themselves; that empowering, in turn, provides them with the strength to take on even greater challenges.

One passage from the Christian scriptures I use frequently

in this context comes from chapter three of Acts of the Apostles in the New Testament. I wrote about this briefly in my autobiography, *Unbowed*, but it is worth going into more depth here. As the story goes, Jesus' disciples Peter and John are walking in the environs of the temple in Jerusalem when a crippled man, who is carried every day on a stretcher into the temple, stretches out his hand to them to beg for money. "I have no silver or gold," Peter says to the beggar, "but what I have I give you; in the name of Jesus Christ of Nazareth, stand up and walk." The passage continues: "And he took him by the right hand and raised him up; and immediately his feet and ankles were made strong" (Acts 3:2–8).

The story recognizes that special qualities and talents, such as those that Peter possesses, can be used for social uplift, and that sometimes the poor or weak *do* need assistance, that they cannot necessarily always help themselves on their own. Indeed, the passage suggests, to quote Luke 12:48, "From everyone to whom much has been given, much will be required; and from one to whom much has been entrusted, even more will be demanded." In other words, it is appropriate that Peter and John are using their God-given skills and gifts in the service of others.

However, what I also appreciate in this story is that Peter and John don't fulfill the beggar's request for money; they recognize that simple charity is not enough. They ask the beggar to *do* something, even though he's been crippled since birth and has been lying on a stretcher every day in the temple for many years. It's up to him, the apostles make clear, to stand up and walk. True, Peter reaches out a hand, but the recipient is asked to exercise a degree of self-determination. The book of Acts says that once the formerly crippled man was cured, he went around praising God. While we cannot be sure what happened next, I highly doubt that he went back to his old ways and begged. The narrative suggests that he was made whole and empowered. He may also have inspired and empowered others in turn through his faith.

One can speculate that it's likely the beggar's problems weren't all solved that day. He still had to find a job; indeed, he may have been earning a small but steady income begging for money. His expectations may now have been raised; he may have believed that now that he'd been made physically able, wealth and happiness would equally miraculously fall into his lap. They probably didn't; they usually don't. Like billions of others, the man would still have had to work to achieve his goals; perhaps he may have had to labor even harder, since he didn't have an illness to provide an excuse, either for himself or for society. This would have required as much of a commitment to and belief in self-betterment as that initial act that led him to reach out his own hand and lift himself to his feet.

Of course, the thrust of this story theologically concerns the power of the faith in Jesus Christ that the two disciples possess, and the miracles they were able to accomplish following their experience of divine inspiration known as Pentecost. However, to me the story of Peter and John and the beggar also contains unmistakable messages of social uplift and personal responsibility. Through these messages I see spiritual values assisting in healing our wounds and the earth's, whether these values are practiced by the rural poor in Africa or elsewhere, or by the relatively well-off in industrialized nations.

The miracle described in Acts is the first to occur after Pentecost. Before this transformative moment, all four of the canonical Gospels have been at pains to stress how ordinary and indeed frail are the disciples who gather around Jesus. Not only does Peter betray Jesus three times on the night before he is crucified, but he and the other disciples fail to stay awake as Jesus prays that night in the Garden of Gethsemane. Throughout Jesus' ministry, the disciples are portrayed in the Gospels as obtuse and fearful, or competitive and argumentative with one another. Indeed, so entrenched are these men's reputations as unsophisticated artisans from the countryside that when they are visited by the tongues of flame and begin speaking eloquently in foreign languages, the crowd in Jerusalem can scarcely believe it: "Are not all these who are speaking Galileans? And how is it that we hear, each of us, in our own native language?" So unlikely is it that these men could be so transformed, that the cosmopolitan crowd assembled for the feast of Passover assumes the followers of Christ must be drunk (Acts 2:7–8, 13).

Nonetheless, the Gospels also make clear that one doesn't have to be visited by divine inspiration either to better oneself or to lead. The call to make sure that one capitalizes on the opportunities and gifts that God has provided one with is an undeniable feature of Jesus' ministry. In the Parable of the Talents (Matt. 25:14–30; Luke 19:12–28), for instance, two servants are given five and two coins (or "talents") respectively by their master and told to use them wisely. They invest their talents and receive, in interest, five and two more in return. A third servant, on the other hand, who has been entrusted with a single coin, buries his, too fearful of his master or too ignorant of monetary matters to do anything with it. The master praises the two servants who have doubled what they were given, and chastises the one who hasn't. He takes the only talent that the poorest man has and gives it to the one who has made the most.

This parable makes it clear that not everyone has the same capacities, to use the contemporary meaning of the word "talent." Indeed, human beings are like a forest, in which some trees are tall and others are short, although all serve their purpose in the ecosystem and all can flourish in different ways. However, I find the parable useful because it suggests that one is obligated to use what one has been given to the best of one's ability. Should you squander the aptitude or resources you have, or fail to develop them in a productive way, then whatever else you have will be taken from you, too, and given to someone who has best used what he was given. We can almost literally observe this today in our own societies: the rich get richer, and the poor get poorer.

In the many discussions I have with women and men in Green Belt groups, I draw on the Parable of the Talents to make clear that one can have few possessions and still maintain one's self-respect; likewise, while one may not be proud of one's poverty, one can be proud of oneself as a person. Taking a lesson from the Benedictines, I add that one can also be proud of one's work, or what one can produce or grow or repair with one's own hands.

Of course, because its aim is principally theological, this

parable doesn't acknowledge the inherent inequity that exists between the master and his servants—called "slaves" in some translations. It doesn't examine why the servants have so little and the master has so much to give in the first place. Clearly, systemic injustices make it hard for the poor to escape their poverty and easy for the rich, in both wealthy and poor countries, to become even wealthier.

Because of that inequity, the Green Belt Movement has long combined practical programs to plant trees, restore degraded landscapes and forests, improve food security, harvest water, reduce waste, and launch and maintain sustainable enterprises, with campaigns for good governance as essential tools for social, economic, and ecological transformation. "Good governance" means that leaders are held accountable for their actions, that they make decisions openly and transparently, and that they are committed to using the resources at their disposal (financial, human, and environmental) equitably and responsibly.

Nonetheless, anyone, no matter how disadvantaged socially or economically, or how unjust his circumstances, can better himself, or lift himself up and walk. This has been a central message of the GBM's work. And over the decades, hundreds of thousands of people have, through community tree-planting networks, proved it to be true. Self-empowerment is an essential element if the struggle to heal the earth's wounds, and our own, is to succeed. For that self-empowerment to come about, the church has a crucial role to play and the faithful have a responsibility to God's creation. As Pope Benedict XVI indicated in his letter "If You Want to Cultivate Peace, Protect Creation," written for the celebration of World Day of Peace

2010 and quoting from the catechism of the Catholic Church: "Respect for creation is of immense consequence, not least because 'creation is the beginning and the foundation of all God's works,' and its preservation has now become essential for the peaceful coexistence of mankind."

CHAPTER EIGHT

Self-Knowledge

In Kenya, *kesha* is a popular activity for many Christians. It's an all-night Pentecostal vigil during which the faithful pray, drum, and sing to appeal to God to intercede on their behalf. People believe that if they pray and drum loudly and long enough, God may turn his attention to them and provide them with riches, fame, or whatever they desire. In spite of the display of energy and dedication for hours on end, there's a disheartening passivity embedded in this practice, even though the praying, drumming, and singing can get very spirited. It's as if people are forsaking all belief in their own ability to bring about the change they would like to see in their lives. Instead of, for example, taking strength from their faith to empower themselves, they are leaving all the power—all the agency—in God's hands.

It is the Green Belt Movement's vision to urge individuals not to wait for divine intervention, but to give themselves the energy they imagine, or pray that God will provide, and to recognize that God expects them to take action and rise up and walk! Indeed, through its work and seminars, the Green Belt Movement asks individuals why they take for granted the bountiful resources with which the Creator has endowed them. Why do they cut down the trees, and watch the rain God has provided run off and wash away the soil that God provided for agriculture, into the streams or rivers that God provided, and then out to the sea, which God also provided? To refer to the passage from Acts of the Apostles again, the environment is, in effect, the fingers on the hand that God has been stretching out to them for decades, hoping that they will grasp it and lift themselves up, as the beggar did with Peter and John. But the people have been batting the hand away, too intent on joining their own hands together in prayer or flaying the skins on the drums through the night, to cherish God's creation that's right in front of them.

During the civic and environmental seminars, it is sometimes necessary to remind people of how ignorance about their environment has profoundly disturbing consequences. In the words of Hosea: "Hear the word of the Lord, O people of Israel; for the Lord has an indictment against the inhabitants of the land," laments the prophet.

> There is no faithfulness or loyalty, or knowledge of God in the land. Swearing, lying, murder, and stealing and adultery break out; bloodshed follows bloodshed. Therefore the land mourns, and all who live in it languish; together with the wild animals and the birds of the air, even the fish of the sea are perishing. . . . My people are destroyed for lack of knowledge (Hosea 4:1–4, 6).

When we discuss this and other passages, we ask the seminar participants: "Why do you think that God would tell the children of Israel, through their prophet, that they will die because of their ignorance? Why do you think that if you do not take care of the soil, but allow it to wash away because you haven't dug terraces or trenches to harvest rainwater for your crops, or if you haven't saved money to buy manure or fertilizer and your seeds fail because the ground is weak, God will do it for you? Is that not ignorance on your part?" We frequently use the words of the great prophets of the Hebrew scriptures—Hosea, Jeremiah, and Isaiah among them—to speak across the centuries and the continents directly to us and many of those with whom we work.

Isaiah cries out: "The earth dries up and withers; the world languishes and withers. . . . The earth lies polluted under its inhabitants; for they have transgressed laws, violated the statutes, broken the everlasting covenant" (Isa. 24:4–5). This may seem harsh, but sometimes it's important for people to hear the truth, no matter how tough it is, if they are going to be shocked out of their passivity, *know* themselves, and then better their situation. By acknowledging our own destructiveness, we have an opportunity to remedy it. But we can't keep hoping that God will come and rectify our mistakes because we have woken him up or drummed him into action.

For too many religious practitioners, being "good" requires a passive acceptance of suffering in the hope of a reward after death. A popular Buddhist story tells of a man who was a fervent devotee of the Chinese bodhisattva Guan-yin. A bodhisattva is an enlightened being who vows not to be released from the cycle of death, birth, and rebirth that characterizes the Buddhist view of existence until all sentient beings have been relieved of their suffering. One day, runs one modern version of the tale, a great flood comes and swamps the devotee's house, forcing him to take to the second floor.

As he looks out the window and prays to Guanyin to appear in all her radiant glory and rescue him, a man comes by on a boat.

"Jump in," he says. "I will take us to dry land."

"No, I'm okay," replies the devotee. "Guanyin will rescue me."

The man rows away, and still the waters rise, until the devotee is forced onto the roof of his house. As the devotee prays once more to Guanyin, another man comes by in a boat.

"Why don't you get in?" asks this man. "The flood is still rising and you haven't much time."

"No, thank you," replies the devotee. "Guanyin always promises to rescue those who worship her. She will come to my aid."

The man rows away, and still the waters rise, until the water has risen to the devotee's neck. Finally, a helicopter appears and a ladder is lowered to the man. "Reach out your hand and climb up!" shouts a man from inside the helicopter.

But the devotee is adamant. Indeed, he remains so sure that Guanyin will rescue him that when he drowns and goes to the world beyond this one, he remonstrates with the spirits as to why, after a life of selfless and committed prayer and devotion to Guanyin, who'd vowed to save all sentient beings, she'd forgotten him in his hour of need.

"What do you mean 'forgotten'?" replies one of the spirits. "Didn't she send people in two boats and a helicopter to rescue you?"

This story has many morals—that divine providence takes many forms; that our community around us offers us examples of holiness in action; that we should not keep waiting for miracles to occur when human agency may be all that is needed; that we would be foolish to squander the opportunities that are right in front of us in favor of the highly unlikely one-in-a-million chance. They go to the heart of this third value of self-knowledge at the center of the GBM's work. The manifestations of faith shown by the devotee of Guanyin are not only deeply injurious to individuals, but by the individuals refusing to accept their own agency as they wait to be saved by someone else, whether in this lifetime or beyond, a very destructive disempowerment within communities is encouraged.

One disturbing consequence of this disempowerment is that those in authority (including the clergy) can use that passivity for their own ends. The trust that the faithful place in their religious leaders puts an extra burden of responsibility on the latter. For this reason, given the overwhelming evidence of serious ecological challenges, including climate change, I would hope that every preacher, imam, rabbi, guru, sensei, and priest would balance making sure we gain some surety over what happens after we die with an equal insistence on the preservation of the earth and our particular accountability for the survival of the planet's ecosystems: that we are not simply "passing through," as the Jim Reeves song states. When we do pass, we shall leave the planet to our children and our grandchildren.

How refreshing and empowering it would be to enter a church or a mosque or other place of worship and hear about those who have been inspired to change the conditions under which they labor outside of the building, by making sure that natural resources were used accountably, responsibly, and equitably! How inspiring it would be to hear from religious leaders who can explain to their congregations and communities throughout the Congo, for instance, that their trees have value beyond that which the timber companies, traders, and governmental representatives may be telling them. That they *can* protect what God has given them and not turn it into charcoal!

Unfortunately, many Christian churches are burdened with a historical legacy of being bulwarks against change. In the case of the plantations owned by churches in the Caribbean in the eighteenth and nineteenth centuries, the wealth was made from the trade in, and the slave labor of, human beings themselves. Throughout Africa in the nineteenth and twentieth centuries, missionaries worked with colonialists to undermine the confidence of local peoples. As institutions, churches reaped enormous financial gains from the ownership of land and property. Many still own substantial tracts of land and are very wealthy. Indeed, in many African countries, land policies cannot be changed to benefit the poor without forcibly taking large tracts from church organizations.

To be sure, many parishioners genuinely find the church to be a place of consolation for the challenges they face in their lives, of hope amid despair. It can provide valuable spiritual and psychological comfort, especially to people who are poor and disenfranchised. But churches can also put significant burdens on such people. In Kenya, many rural congregants on Sundays will rise early, leave home with only a cup of tea for breakfast, and walk to church, which can be a good distance away. The service can last for four hours, even though some congregants may be old or very young, and most haven't eaten anything all day. Parishioners will also have been expected to contribute to at least one, and sometimes several, collections during the service. Often they are told that the money they donate will be returned to them in blessings and even enrichment from God. Instead of "Rise up and walk!" the message is "Rise up and pay!"

Lamentations about the greed and corruption of institutions of religion have been common through the centuries. They are unique neither to Africa nor to Christianity. Yet it remains dispiriting when the church appears to side with the powerful against the powerless, and demands of the poor more money than they can afford. Of course, Jesus himself had to contend with religious authorities more interested in their own reputation and expressions of piety than genuine concern for the spiritual life or the lot of the indigent or distressed (see Matt. 3:7). But it is still sad when an institution in which so many place their last hope and trust demands more than the poor can afford and continues to let them down.

Perhaps the church should be in the business of trying to challenge its parishioners' awareness and raising their consciousnesses rather than asking from them more than they can give. Faith traditions today ought to be in the forefront of protecting God's creation. One would hope that those in religious authority recognize that whatever we might consider "heaven" (a paradisal state where the burdens of life are alleviated) or "hell" (where those burdens are amplified to the point of being unbearable) both exist, and that it is our responsibility to bring about heaven and reduce the presence of hell on Earth today.

Yet sometimes the opposite is the case: religious leaders are promoting activities that cause more wounds to the earth and to individuals. For instance, it is possible for a poor woman in Kenya to cut the last tree she has on her land and make it into charcoal, so that she has something material with a monetary value to give to the church on the following Sunday. Or she might wait for the lone chicken she has to lay the last egg, so she can take it as an offering, even though she or her young children may need it more than the priest does.

In the past, those chosen to be the mediators between the human and divine worlds in traditional cultures (as in my Kikuyu community) had very different relationships with their congregations. They worked for their material wealth, and didn't live off their fellow citizens, who weren't expected to support the priest. The elders would determine what needed to be sacrificed to God (a goat, for example), and whichever elder had the chosen creature would consider himself blessed. The elders would not pay for the goat; rather it was the "chosen" elder's way of giving back to God. Unfortunately, some priests, when asked today why the clergy or elders of the church can't earn their own living—either with formal jobs or at least raising livestock or crops, instead of relying on the faithful to feed them—reply: "Our job is to preach." How can talking every day of the week be a full-time job? Surely, there is something wrong about a vision of a God, and a church, where healthy and able-bodied men and women are satisfied with being supported by congregants who are often desperately poor.

It's fair to ask what spiritual resources could be used to gather the courage and strength to take a stand against what one sees as wrong. Perhaps it is attaining a level of consciousness that does not allow one to feel peace with oneself if something is being done that seems unjust. That same awareness can give you a resolve so that you are not overwhelmed. Instead, you feel empowered to take action and gradually it becomes possible to figure out what to do.

Most activists don't have a blueprint they consult each morning when they wake up. Most begin by learning, then working, then learning more, then gaining inspiration, and if they're lucky, receiving encouragement from those around them. You can't always anticipate what will inspire you, what will raise your consciousness to the necessary level, or how this consciousness will inspire other people. Simply recognizing that a problem exists can be an important part of the process of awakening.

Another one is focus. When I was about eight or nine, I caught my mother looking down at nothing in particular that I could see. All I could discern was that she was very focused, to the point that it was as if she didn't even realize that I sat right there beside her, watching her curiously. I looked exactly at the point at which she was looking and tried to focus as she did. Every time I looked up at her, however, she was still focused on the same spot. I, of course, had lost my focus. Soon I

went off and entertained myself with something more interest-
ing, and forgot my mother and her state. As an adult, though,
I've often recalled that moment, as I catch myself focusing so
intently that I do not see or hear what is happening around
me. Something like this happens not because we force it to,
but because of the intensity of our accumulated experiences.
As a child, I really didn't have anything to focus on so intently.
As an adult, however, I find there is much—almost *too* much—
that commands my total attention.

When we consider self-knowledge and self-betterment—
that capacity to use our talents and make a difference in our
lives and the lives of those around us—we often think of the
words "vocation" or "mission." These terms evoke the spiritual
life, and that's appropriate, for they represent a calling that
goes beyond our own narrow interests.

Sometimes I'm asked what advice I would give to people
who feel lost and are searching for their calling or mission in
life and want to become involved in environmental causes.
They may care about the earth but haven't yet found a way to
take action. They doubt their abilities, or don't know on which
challenge to focus: climate change, species extinction, lack of
clean water, deforestation, spreading deserts, industrial pollution, overconsumption and waste, coral bleaching, or the lack
of green spaces in urban centers, for example.

I counsel them not to despair. As far as I'm concerned,
even if you haven't found what seems like the right focus for
your energy, you should continue what you're doing, but bring
passion to it. That passion may help you discover what's inside
yourself, and lead you to what you really want to do, what

really encourages that deep attention. As I suggested earlier, the task that reveals itself to you doesn't have to be great. Could you advocate for your city or local municipality to provide more open spaces for playgrounds and parks? Could you demand more bike paths and wider sidewalks to encourage people to exercise more and leave their cars behind? Could you encourage your schools to adopt healthier diets sourced from local farmers? Perhaps suggest that teachers and children leave the classroom more to learn about the natural world by working in school garden plots or helping clean up trash or studying animals in their local habitat? Why not volunteer to clean up the trash in a nearby neighborhood, or talk in your local school about why you think the environment is important? Why not watch birds and listen to their songs, or notice spiderwebs on branches, or listen to the flowing waters in a nearby stream?

If you sit and wait for inspiration, as I did as a child watching my mother, nothing may happen. But keep busy working and something will come your way. It's important to find what inspires you, what helps you move from what I call a "fixed state" into an energetic mode. Sometimes you need to be out of your comfort zone, to experience or learn about people or problems far removed from your own life. Sometimes, though, you need to give yourself a Sabbath—to step back, and in effect replenish yourself before you can better yourself and the earth.

The truth is, sometimes our minds need a rest. Even rivers, which can flow with torrential force, reach a wetland area where the waters slow down and move in circles. As they swirl around, the waters also follow channels that lead to underground reservoirs and fill them. It may seem that the river is simply meandering and stagnating, but wetlands can be very fertile areas that provide a lot of life and clean water. So it is with moments of reflection. Give yourself time to think and find your direction once again; allow your own reserves of energy to be replenished through time in the natural world. You don't have to have a particular place of solace in nature. Perhaps you feel the need to disappear into a forest or a cave, but a park or just sitting on a riverbank can serve, too. In fact, anything can capture our attention: a bird, a fruit on a tree, a flower, watching a river flow; just being quiet. It is refreshing to know that life is everywhere.

If it isn't possible to spend time in nature, then you can take a vacation, or see a movie, or visit a friend, or do volunteer work. In a break from stimulation and the rush of activities, that's where you can find yourself, and even the source of creativity. It is also possible to find that inspiration, even if the mind is exhausted, by picking up a book. It is as if the person who wrote it is speaking directly to you, focusing your attention. However, if you find your mind wandering from the page, then put the book down and go for a walk—in the direction the spirit leads you.

When you find the work that you're meant to do, it will occupy you so completely that you may feel like you don't have time for anything else. Your calling will pull you forward through the difficult times and give you the strength you didn't think you possessed to overcome hurdles—but you can't always look for and expect to find it. It has to come from deep within you—from your own Source—although it may be triggered by events or circumstances or knowledge or urgent needs outside of you. And it will likely draw from the wellspring of another essential value, a desire to serve and give back.

CHAPTER NINE

The Commitment to Service

The commitment to service is the final important value at the heart of the Green Belt Movement's work, and key to the spiritual and ecological regeneration we seek. Those participating in Green Belt networks receive only a small token of appreciation for planting and sustaining trees. By design, it's not a salary or stipend. We want people to be driven by the understanding of a nonmonetized value: to give their time, energy, and resources, with no expectation of material reward beyond that of being involved in something larger than oneself.

From a spiritual perspective, when we are able to control our craving and instill in ourselves a discipline that tames the greed and selfishness to which we can too easily fall victim, we increase our sense of satisfaction and happiness. We also lose the feeling of "dis-ease" that may be the reason so many desperate people, most distressingly the young, feel the need to medicate and anesthetize themselves with cigarettes, drugs, and alcohol.

One dimension of service that I feel strongly about is the principle of servant leadership. In *The Challenge for Africa,* I explored examples of individuals who helped their communities by dedicating themselves to assisting the development of all its members, no matter their social or economic status. Such leadership was, of course, evident in the ministry of prophets and saints. Jesus, for one, modeled how to serve. He offered himself and his message to those on the margins of his society: the poor, the outcasts, women, even beggars. Jesus' ministry was the opposite of self-service: it did not create victims of predatory leadership that exploits the vulnerability of its followers.

Selfless service is the basis for much of what we admire in those we see as exemplars of what is best in humanity—people who represent a model of not only self-empowerment but also of how to motivate others to act for the common good. These models are found in the realm of politics (among individuals such as Nelson Mandela, Julius Nyerere of Tanzania, and the leaders of Kenya's fighters for independence, the best known of whom is Dedan Kimathi Waciuri); in campaigns for civil and human rights (Mahatma Gandhi, Rev. Martin Luther King, Jr., and earlier champions who fought against slavery and colonialism); and among those who championed the dignity of the poor and dispossessed (Dorothy Day of the *Catholic Worker,* Mother Teresa of Calcutta, and the Brazilian environmentalist and union leader Chico Mendes, who was slain in 1988).

I also see such a dedication in Archbishop Oscar Romero of El Salvador, who was assassinated in 1980 for speaking out on behalf of the victims of the civil war in his country; Father Jerzy Popieluszko, who was kidnapped and killed in 1984, because of his support for the Polish trade union Solidarity; and the American nun Dorothy Stang, who was murdered in Brazil in 2005 while defending the rights of the landless and the protection of rain forest. I am inspired by my fellow Nobel laureate Aung San Suu Kyi of Burma for continuing to stand up for what is just, even when the most fundamental human rights have been denied to her. Because of the force of their example, sometimes at the cost of their own lives, all of these individuals have allowed other ordinary people to stand with them and accomplish extraordinary deeds.

In moments when we feel challenged, we would do well to remember such heroes and others like them, who have made a commitment to service, and the struggles they endured—many of them motivated by their faith tradition. As a student in the United States in the 1960s, I saw the affluent postwar society attempting to come to terms with the long-term injustices of racial discrimination and segregation. Civil rights leaders such as Dr. King, Rev. Ralph Abernathy, and Rev. Joseph Lowery of the Southern Christian Leadership Conference drew on long-standing religious themes—such as the Exodus narrative of the Israelites' escape from slavery—as well as the established network of black churches to call for freedom and equity for the downtrodden and disenfranchised. The success of these black heroes in the United States in turn inspired a new generation of leadership in the African diaspora, where people realized that they, too, could liberate themselves from colonialism and discrimination on their own continents and in their own regions.

It is easy to forget, more than half a century after this work began, how radical and even unsettling was Dr. King's call for justice. His message was not simply a demand for recompense for wrongs committed against people of color. It contained a commitment to solidarity with the poor of all colors and nations. I saw how inspired ordinary people were by this message and how they maintained their human dignity in the face of insults, attack dogs, water cannons, police batons, bombings, and assassinations, drawing in large measure upon their faith. Here was an example of both leaders and ordinary people working together for the greater good of their community and future generations.

I took this inspiration back to Kenya, and have drawn upon the legacy of the civil rights movement in our own people's struggles to combat injustice. In this effort, people of faith played their parts. Indeed, several members of the clergy have stood with the people against powerful interests and spoken out, for example, against the imprisonment, torture, displacement, and outright murder or extra-judicial killings of opponents of the autocratic regime. Among those leaders, all of whom faced tangible risks to their physical safety and their position, were Archbishop Ndingi Mwana'a Nzeki, now emeritus Catholic archbishop of Nairobi; Bishop Alexander Kipsang Muge of the Anglican Church; and Rev. Timothy Njoya of the Presbyterian Church of East Africa. In 1992, Rev. Peter Njenga, then provost of the Anglican All Saints Cathedral in Nairobi, allowed me and mothers of political prisoners to seek sanctuary in the cathedral's crypt. Later, Rev. Njenga became one of the few priests who embraced the Green Belt Movement's call to plant trees on Easter Monday.

For their selfless service, some of these individuals paid the ultimate price. Father John Kaiser, a priest from Minnesota, was murdered in 2000 by unknown assailants in Morendat, Kenya, not only for standing up to the fomenting of ethnic violence as a policy of the government, but for providing sanctuary to two young girls who'd allegedly been raped by a government minister. When Father Kaiser appealed to the government to help the girls, police instead overran the offices where the girls were sheltered. He was shot in the head and his body dumped along the roadside. A decade earlier, Bishop Muge was warned that if he didn't stop condemning the policies of the then government, including the instigation of a series of lethal ethnic clashes, he should fear for his life. The then labor minister publicly stated that if Muge entered his parliamentary constituency, Busia, in western Kenya, where the violence was rife, Muge "might not leave alive." Muge defied the warning. On his way home from Busia, his car collided with a milk truck—a fatal "accident" such as that which occurred to too many opposition figures, including members of civil society, and defenders of human rights during this dark period in Kenyan history.

These individuals and others, both religious and lay, too many to mention, acted out of the generosity of their hearts and were strengthened by their belief in a power greater than their own. They undertook tasks for the community as a whole and struggled for something more than simply their own material gain or social empowerment. They worked for the common good because they embraced the value of service. There are, of course, countless others like them in every region. They haven't sought recognition, and haven't garnered acclaim or headlines. Quite often, nobody even notices them. They come, they serve, and they go.

In addition to the civil rights movement, I was also inspired by liberation theology, another embodiment of the value of service to emerge from the Christian tradition in the 1960s.

Some sources assign its origination to Gustavo Gutiérrez Merino, a Peruvian Dominican priest of indigenous (Quechua) ancestry, who found in the Bible a "preferential option for the poor." This latter principle was formulated by Latin American priests in 1968 and articulated by Gutiérrez in his 1973 book, *A Theology of Liberation.* It found in Jesus' ministry a commitment to associate and side with the marginalized in society.

Liberation theology considered poverty itself to be a sin, and liberation theologians declared that the church had, in many ways, held the faithful captive by serving political and economic systems that exploited and dehumanized the poor. Priests came to the fore to demand that governments be held accountable for their actions and be sensitive to the lives of the poor, who had so little say in how their societies were organized and managed. Liberation theologians and members of religious orders also declared that the church should be helping people to free themselves from oppressive structures. It should instill in them a belief in their right to and capacity for self-betterment; that ordinary people need to be empowered and encouraged not to accept as divinely ordained the political and economic reality where a few individuals own a huge percentage of the resources and the masses are held captive in poverty.

Liberation theology was controversial, principally because its critics linked its concern for social justice and the social and political conditions under which the poor labored to a Marxist ideology that encouraged notions of the redistribution of wealth or even revolution. However, I was intrigued and inspired by its ideas — not least because I saw how it emphasized that ordinary people needed to organize themselves to find solutions to their own problems, and to do so in a way that encouraged an ethic of community. It was also, I believed, a powerful way to respond to injustice through nonviolence, and thus struck me as being in line with the prophetic tradition of speaking truth to power while simultaneously promoting genuine peace based on equity.

Although priests who advocated liberation theology were sanctioned by the church, some priests and congregations in Latin America continue to advocate its principles. In the meantime, Latin America has seen improvements in its systems of governance and in the redistribution of wealth. Many societies in the region have moved from the dictatorships, state violence, violations of human rights, and stark inequalities that characterized the region in the 1970s and 1980s, and have made progress in alleviating poverty and supporting human development. It would seem that this is in part due to the contribution of the values embedded within liberation theology.

Of course, injustice and poverty remain, and why they still do and how to address them are challenges for every generation. Likewise, how the religious should relate to the political and economic social structures in which they find themselves is an age-old debate within faith traditions. Jesus told his disciples that he would not be with them all the time, but the poor always would (Matt. 26:11), and that they should separate their worldly responsibilities from the commitments of their faith (Matt. 22:21). However, Jesus would have expected secular or religious institutions to try to lessen poverty and privation, and work to eliminate them altogether. The misery, pain, and economic stagnation that affect so many poor people—especially in Africa, where Christianity is growing rapidly—should gnaw at the conscience of the religious and politicians alike. The belief that God ordains all leaders is not a part of liberation theology: for how, its proponents ask, can God ordain a murderer and a torturer?

I remain hopeful that, especially in sub-Saharan Africa, religion will become a liberatory experience. Some priests and other religious in Africa do agree with the tenet of a "preferential option for the poor," and continue to struggle to end the passivity so many Christians in Africa have been taught is their Christian obligation. Looking at the example of the nuns and priests who shaped the path of those of us who went on to seek change, I see there was such a commitment to serve, to live for others, and working for the common good. Their light can be multiplied as many times as there are faithful men and women of goodwill on earth.

How might Christian spirituality and a commitment to service manifest itself in caring for the earth? Because Christianity in the past has woven itself into the colonization and exploitation of many parts of the world, the political dominion of the powerful has tended to go hand in hand with dominion over the earth rather than custodianship of it. Some in Christian history have resisted this: Francis of Assisi (1182–1226), founder of the Franciscan Order, was not only concerned for the environment and the other species with which we share the planet, but he was an early proponent of interfaith dialogue. With Clare of Assisi (1194–1253), founder of the Poor Clares, Francis also ministered, and gave a preferential option to the poor. Both were from privileged backgrounds, yet they refused to use their positions and wealth to advance their own interests and instead dedicated themselves to service. They and other saints I learned about as a girl stood up for the poor at a time when to do so wasn't easy (one could argue it never has been).

In tandem with the emergence of liberation theology, Christian theologians have been attempting to reclaim what they see as the forgotten ethos of care for creation and ecological justice that runs through the tradition. Among the most influential and vital of the voices calling for greater ecological consciousness among Christians is the late American Passionist priest Thomas Berry (1914–2009). Berry developed what he called the "New Story" of creation, one in which human beings embraced a reciprocal relationship with the earth and one another, instead of one based on dominion or exploitation. "The universe is a communion of subjects, not a collection of objects," Berry declared, and the earth a commons where "each individual being is supported by every other being in the earth community. In turn, each being contributes to the well-being of every other being in the community."[1]

When I first heard Berry speak, I was gratified. Here was a priest in the vanguard of the environmental movement, even as I was lamenting the fact that for the most part, those in religious orders weren't at the forefront of raising awareness of the importance of the environment, but rather trailing along at the back.

Because of his and others' work, growing awareness of the centrality of the earth to humans' existence, and the threats to it, hasn't been wholly ignored by Christian denominations. The World Council of Churches, for example, has for decades examined environmental and social justice issues. A recent project on the links between poverty, wealth, and ecology encourages churches to find alternatives to the prevailing model of economic globalization that exerts huge environmental costs, among them deforestation, resource exploitation, and climate change.

In 1990, Pope John Paul II's World Peace Day message was entitled "Peace with God the Creator—Peace with All of Creation." In it, he acknowledged that one of the realities threatening world peace was "a lack of due respect for nature." "A new ecological awareness is beginning to emerge which," he continued, "rather than being downplayed, ought to be encouraged to develop into concrete programs and initiatives." His successor, Pope Benedict XVI, has said, "Our earth speaks to us, and we must listen if we want to survive."

I have seen this commitment to service and the environment among Christians of several denominations in my own country. As far back as 1992, for instance, when he was a bishop, Archbishop David Mukuba Gitari of the Anglican Church invited me to celebrate World Environment Day with him and to plant a tree with him in the compound of his church. In 1999, he joined the Green Belt Movement's campaign to protect Karura Forest in the north of Nairobi from being despoiled by land-grabbers and private developers. Archbishop Gitari marched with us and exposed himself to physical danger from the thugs hired to stop us from protesting and planting trees, because he was committed to the protection of God's creation. Archbishop Gitari, together with Archbishop Ndingi and Rev. Mutava Musyimi, the general secretary of the National Council of Churches of Kenya, blessed twenty-three seedlings in a service in Uhuru Park in downtown Nairobi on behalf of protecting the forest.

Even liberation theology, which didn't begin with an environmental consciousness, has become more aware. In the 1990s, the Brazilian liberation theologian Leonardo Boff effectively summarized a key tenet of the Green Belt Movement: that "social injustice leads to ecological injustice, and vice versa." He reminded Christians that in addition to human poverty, the rupture between human beings and the environment was itself a sin.[2]

Pioneered in the United States, the environmental justice movement grew out of the concerns that highly polluting facilities such as chemical factories, garbage collecting points, landfills, and bus depots were being sited disproportionately in neighborhoods with large concentrations of people of color who were also more economically disadvantaged. Organizations such as WE ACT for Environmental Justice in New York, headed by Peggy Shepard, have been at the forefront of this movement.

Many faith-based organizations have also championed the tenets of the environmental justice movement, including the National Council of Churches Eco-Justice Program, the National Religious Partnership for the Environment, as well as many individual Catholic churches.

Denominations within Judaism and Protestantism, as well as the Roman Catholic Church, have emphasized that the earth belongs to God and not to mankind; that we are the stewards of creation and should not be its exploiters; and that human dignity and a commitment to the poor are fundamental to the sustainable use of the planet's resources. Some denominations are actively encouraging the greening of churches and other places of worship.

Indeed, the motif of the Jubilee in the Jewish tradition offers a very concrete and practical example of how environmental conservation (in the form of letting the ground lie fallow and the animals rest from their labors) is tied to economic and social action (the redistribution of land and the forgiving of debts) and broader attempts to bring the community together. It exemplifies why any of our individual efforts to act responsibly with our precious natural resources or any of our collective attempts, for instance, to conserve energy and find alternatives to fossil fuels, cannot be divorced from an equally forceful commitment to social justice.

The Green Belt Movement's work has embraced environmental justice, in its belief that all human beings have a right to a clean and healthy environment. We all seek it, but it is often only the wealthy who have the means to create and enforce that right. Those who are poor or marginalized don't have the same options. For instance, they may live in an environment where they are forced to drink filthy, unhygienic water, even as others can sample the purest water in the world, whether it's piped to their homes and filtered, or bought in bottles. This inequality is also a wound, not only because it's unfair, but for the pragmatic reason that if an unhealthy environment of a poor urban community is not restored, it will affect not only that community's children but ultimately others', too: a healthy Earth nurtures healthy populations.

As the effects of global warming become more evident, the environmental justice movement has itself globalized to become a campaign for climate justice. To some extent, climate change is like any other environmental challenge, except on a worldwide scale. The environmental justice movement recognizes that the environmental costs of industrialization are borne disproportionately by the poor, and seeks to rectify that injustice. In the same manner, climate justice campaigners argue that the poorer countries will be most adversely affected by climate change and that industrialized countries have a moral responsibility to recompense the developing world for their greenhouse gas emissions, or to help these countries avoid the worst consequences of global warming. In the case of Africa, the question can be asked baldly: Is it fair for the African people to die for something they haven't participated much at all in creating?

Climate justice advocates understand that it's not as if those in developed countries deliberately fostered climate change. Moreover, the wealth that has been generated and progress that has been made because of the industrial revolution have been remarkable; it is a path the rest of the world wants to follow. However, an injustice does exist (even if not a deliberate one) and needs to be corrected. Industrialized nations need to stop pumping greenhouse gases into Earth's atmosphere at the current rates, and create a financial mechanism to assist developing nations in adapting to an increasingly erratic climate.

This latter element is crucial. As with Peter and John in Acts of the Apostles, equity doesn't only mean being provided with a helping hand. It means that vulnerable countries need to embrace their own responsibility for mitigating the adverse effects of global warming by, for example, protecting and restoring their own forests and promoting the use of green energy (with technical and financial assistance from industrialized nations). They have every reason to do this, and not to put their sole attention on the financial flows expected to come their way.

Both the environmental justice movement and religious organizations have more recently incorporated the concept of climate justice into their work, and have independently issued statements and declarations that call upon their religious traditions to become actively involved in solving the climate crisis. In 2008, for instance, ninety Catholic bishops from the Northern and Southern hemispheres signed a statement that included this declaration: "It is our moral obligation to take urgent action to tackle climate change and to do so in support of those most affected." Whether independently of liberation theology or inspired by it, the commitment to justice that numerous Christians find at the heart of Holy Scripture has moved to the center of concern in many parts of the world. These are hopeful signs, not least because they can help redeem the past legacy of Christianity as a partner in the subjugation of communities and nations, and perhaps engage its leaders in the forefront of the struggle to seek justice and replenish the earth.

CHAPTER TEN

Spirituality Meets Activism

Throughout the United Nations' climate summit held in Copenhagen in December 2009, I thought about the values I have explored in this book and about the need to move beyond the thinking that seeks to monetize every phenomenon. Can we really put a price tag on the carbon dioxide trees capture? I know scientists and economists are working out such valuations and I wouldn't stop them. But the answer surely is that what they provide is literally incalculable.

I wondered, though, to what extent spiritual values were embraced by the government delegates meeting day and night at Copenhagen's Bella conference center trying to hammer out a new, legally binding agreement to reverse the growth of greenhouse gas emissions. How many of them would champion the inclusion of values such as compassion or empathy in the text? What about justice or equity? Could they even hear these terms if their focus was principally on the money involved?

At a gathering held during the climate summit of spiritual leaders from Christian, Buddhist, Hindu, and other traditions, I asked those in the audience to listen to the voice of the Source as it spoke through the leaders assembled. I reminded them that what we were being asked to protect was priceless. "We cannot live without other forms of life," I said, "like the forests or green vegetation." As such, we had an obligation to speak up since the trees couldn't speak for themselves, nor could the frogs, although both were being affected by climate change.

During the two weeks of the conference, I heard several words reverberating, including transparency, honesty, accountability, fairness, rights, and responsibilities. At events organized by religious and spiritual leaders I heard other terms expressed, such as compassion, empathy, and mottainai (encompassing respect, gratitude, and not wasting).

They reinforced my view that these spiritual values, more than science and data, might be the basis for a true human partnership among our leaders to achieve their ultimate objectives and avoid the cataclysms of melting polar ice, vanishing permafrost and glaciers, deforestation, erratic and failed rains, prolonged drought, drying-up rivers and lakes, parched landscapes, dying animals, and large populations faced with diseases associated with malnutrition.

Those of us attending the Copenhagen summit, and millions of others following the proceedings around the world, were hopeful that governments would agree on a binding timetable and compliance measures, and ratify a new climate treaty that respects science, history, and justice. They didn't achieve all of that. Nonetheless, I remain optimistic. After all, I have been participating in UN meetings since 1976, when I traveled to the Habitat conference on the world's urban centers in Vancouver, Canada. Delegates there also argued and wrangled over language and money.

No delegation ever leaves a global conference with a perfect document or a perfect financial mechanism to implement it, and Copenhagen in 2009 was no different. But the presence in Denmark of 193 heads of state and government, as well as many spiritual leaders, enlarged the possibility of others raising their consciousness to the point where all of us, government delegates included, could visualize a common ground for a partnership between the industrialized and developing nations to slow climate change: one based on a willingness to be trusting, honest, transparent, and responsible, both to our generation and to those yet to be born.

The meeting in Copenhagen with spiritual leaders was, in many ways, comforting and familiar to me, for in the course of my work, I have found much support from and solidarity with people of faith around the world. I know that many members of religious communities are environmentalists, even if their names or their work aren't well known. Among them, a brother- and sisterhood exists, a bond rooted in shared concerns and values. I feel part of this community, too, even though I do not view myself as a spiritual leader. Because of my Catholic education, my immersion in aspects of Christian doctrine, the use of it in my work with the Green Belt Movement, and my embrace of certain spiritual values, people of faith, and especially my teachers, see in me a kindred spirit and a validation of themselves. It is a relationship I cherish and from which I draw strength.

Indeed, I see the awarding of the Nobel Peace Prize as partly a result of the efforts of religious women to educate me and impart to me the values that can help make a difference in the world. Like me, many nuns were first exposed to the environmental movement in the 1970s and came to appreciate the urgency of healing the earth's wounds. However, as religious, they haven't had the opportunities that I, as a layperson, have had to be in the world. They didn't have the stage I did for digging holes!

Although the Irish Loreto sisters, who ran my high school in Kenya, didn't raise either my classmates or myself to be environmentalists per se, they nonetheless today rightly feel a certain satisfaction about the way I've tried to live my adult life, and a pride in their role as my teachers. I'm grateful for their recognition and their feeling that they are celebrating and working alongside me, as I try to inculcate in others the values they helped instill in their students.

Indeed, the greater awareness of our responsibility toward the planet as a whole has forced religious practitioners and scholars to reexamine their faith traditions and apply critical and exegetical thinking to their sacred texts to determine just what resources lie within them to promote a more just and more ecological vision. It has also forged greater consciousness of *one another's* faiths, and encouraged much-needed interreligious dialogue.

In Assisi, Italy, in 1986, Pope John Paul II convened a gathering of global religious leaders for a world day of prayer for peace. Out of this meeting, and in various parliaments of the world's religions from 1993 to 2009, individuals from many faiths have issued declarations calling for peace, global cooperation, and international understanding. Each of these meetings has had either an explicit or an implicit environmental component. In the United States, ongoing dialogue between faiths and a commitment to peace and the environment has over the years taken place under the auspices of the Temple of Understanding and the Cathedral Church of Saint John the Divine (especially in the 1980s and 1990s during the inspirational leadership of the dean, Rev. James Parks Morton) in New York City; the Center for Respect of Life and the Environment in Washington, D.C.; and Grace Cathedral in San Francisco, among many others.

One admirable result of the ongoing dialogue between scholars and practitioners of different religious traditions was a series of major conferences in the 1990s convened by the Center for the Study of World Religions at Harvard Divinity School, where the spiritual traditions and their relationship with the natural world were examined in detail. These were followed by the publication of nine volumes on the environment and different faith practices under the general editorship of Mary Evelyn Tucker and John Grim, as well as a tenth volume on animals and the world's religions, edited by Paul Waldau and Kimberly Christine Patton. These volumes arguably offer the broadest articulation currently available of the ecological visions and statements found in these world faiths.

Among the many global religious citizens working to promote an environmental consciousness among the different world faiths, Ecumenical Patriarch Bartholomew, Archbishop of Constantinople, the spiritual leader of around three hundred million Orthodox Christians, has been very active in raising awareness and convening meetings with other religious leaders (including issuing a joint statement with Pope John Paul II).

The Iranian scholar Seyyed Hossein Nasr and Jordan's Prince Hassan bin Talal have advocated both greater ecumenical understanding and environmental stewardship from their own Muslim backgrounds.

The Thai activist Sulak Sivaraksa has called for a "socially engaged" Buddhism that embraces the environment within its commitment to peace and alleviating poverty, and Vandana Shiva has drawn upon her Hindu heritage to contest the exploitation of the earth's resources and some of its most vulnerable people. Charles, Prince of Wales, has made environmental conservation a centerpiece of his various interests and has made a commitment in particular to saving the rain forests. For several decades, Satish Kumar, a former Jain monk from India who lives in England, has been popularizing a number of practical ecological approaches from a spiritual perspective through the groundbreaking magazine he founded, *Resurgence.*

Thomas Berry himself was a scholar of Asian religions— including Daoism, Buddhism, and Confucianism—and so acknowledged the great wisdom contained outside the monotheistic traditions. He became an advocate for religious and philosophical pluralism, writing that, "Diversity is no longer something that we tolerate. It is something that we esteem as a necessary condition for a livable universe, as the source of Earth's highest perfection."[1] The U.K.-based Gaia Foundation, whose work was influenced by Thomas Berry, has not only supported the Green Belt Movement but continues to work at the intersection of human rights, ecological consciousness, jurisprudence, and the protection of local peoples' cultures and identities.

The Earth Charter, in whose development the Green Belt

Movement participated, is an important milestone in the application of the tenets of varied spiritual traditions, ethical principles, and values to the cause of protecting the planet. Launched in 2000 in The Hague, the Earth Charter covers a great deal of ground, encompassing virtually every action that human beings take on this planet. Even though it was initiated before climate change was considered to be the problem it is today, the Charter nonetheless remains deeply relevant. Of course, any document is only as good as the understanding of the particular period in which it is written; however, the principles that are espoused are very inclusive, and point to practices that are essential if we are to take the steps needed to mitigate global warming.

The Earth Charter is an encapsulation of much of what we've been trying to achieve through the Green Belt Movement, and unlike an environmental treaty, it is a document that enshrines certain values, important for our survival on the planet.

In addressing how we must respect and care for the community of life, the Earth Charter consciously echoes the principle of "reverence for life," most famously articulated by the German theologian, musician, and physician Albert Schweitzer. Schweitzer rejected the notion of nature as of purely instrumental value and embraced the variety of an ecosystem's living forms and an appreciation that all creation—whether a tree or stream, or the worms in the soil—deserved respect and even reverence.

One of the prime movers of the Earth Charter was Steven Rockefeller, who was a professor at Middlebury College in Vermont. To develop the charter, Steven gathered a number of individuals, among them Mary Evelyn Tucker and John Grim; Susan Davis, who ran the Women's Environment & Development Organization (WEDO); Rabbi Awraham Soetendorp from the Netherlands; the late Kamla Chowdhry, an advisor to the Indian government and many international bodies; Leonardo Boff, the Brazilian liberation theologian; Princess Basma bint Talal of Jordan; and Maurice Strong, the first director of the United Nations Environment Programme.

The Earth Charter was envisioned to enshrine a set of principles for environmental protection of the earth, much as the 1949 Universal Declaration of Human Rights had for the rights of individuals. The idea was drawn from a set of universal spiritual values and gelled at the 1992 "Earth Summit" in Rio de Janeiro, Brazil. Extensive consultation followed, with a broad coalition of groups encompassing faith traditions from around the world—a process that, as you might imagine given the scope of the issues and constituencies involved, identified more and more issues that had to be encompassed. The Earth Charter was ratified; its secretariat, managed by Mirian Vilela, is based in Costa Rica.

Since the Charter's publication, thousands of nongovernmental organizations, schools, businesses, institutions, and religious communities throughout the world have endorsed it. Education is a major area of focus for the Earth Charter Initiative. The Earth Charter Center for Education for Sustainable Development has been established at the University for Peace in Costa Rica and is working to promote the Charter's use in schools, colleges, universities, and nonformal education programs across the world. An Earth Charter School Network has been established and is actively sharing the document; materials have been created to encourage the Charter's use in classrooms; and information has been disseminated on education for sustainable development projects inspired by the Charter.

Hopefully, the Charter will eventually become a basis for environmental education in schools from primary to college, so that young people finish their formal education with an understanding of the planet and with the critical capacity to question their—and their societies'—relationship with Earth and its biological systems.

It is not so important that the logging company I visited in the Congo has read the Earth Charter. Nor does it matter that every businessman and politician uses it as his or her guide. As long as each businessman or politician understands the value and necessity of maintaining an ecosystem's ecological integrity, then, even if he or she has never heard of the Charter, he or she is in some way touching upon the issues with which the Charter is concerned.

To that extent, I was very pleased to learn that Ecuador in 2008 approved a new constitution that incorporates the rights of nature—the first constitution to do so—stating that nature "has the right to exist, persist, maintain and regenerate its vital cycles, structure, functions, and its processes in evolution." As of yet, however, no other country has made a similar commitment, but I have cause to hope that governments will rise to the challenge, even if not necessarily at a constitutional level, to protect the environment both nationally and internationally.

Many people may look with skepticism upon constitutional

amendments, charters, and conventions drafted and announced by governments or international committees, including those promulgated by the United Nations. Even if they are binding, with some kind of international legal statute backing them up, these declarations, resolutions, and proclamations may be ignored or belittled by governments, corporations, and individuals who cynically don't believe they'll be acted on or enforced. And it is true: none of them will mean anything unless people— from the international to the national to the community level— act on them, and those in authority protect the rights and police the demands they establish.

Nonetheless, I believe these aspirational and inspirational documents serve an important purpose of holding up a mirror to the best of our sacred traditions, at the very least providing something of an alternative vision of our faiths than that of granting us a divine mandate to do whatever we wish to the planet, because "life" here is merely transitory and meaningless. Furthermore, these statements also reflect a coming together of a global consensus among religious and spiritual traditions that Earth matters, that what we do during our time on this planet is important, and that we cannot exist in the world as though the coming generations of humans and animals are not entitled to live in it.

For, if nothing else, that we should need these declarations and the Earth Charter at all testifies to a recognition among the peoples of the world that something has gone awry. Indigenous and local peoples who lived close to the land in essentially a preindustrial age did not need a charter with which to understand the natural world. Even though the rules and regulations of their communities were not written down, these peoples had a comprehension of their ecosystems that those of us who are disconnected from the natural environment have lost. In their stated commitment to the indigenous and the poor, therefore, the world's religious declarations and the Earth Charter are in some ways attempts to recognize and support people and communities whose knowledge and wisdom were lost. Recapturing that now may help all of us survive.

CHAPTER ELEVEN

Responding to the Call to Serve

What is it that calls someone to serve, to make that commitment beyond oneself that can transform the lives of those around one and bring about change that had seemed impossible? It could be inspiration, and the knowledge that compels one to act. But sometimes we are called into action on behalf of a cause because of what might be called the god within us, the Source—the voice that we feel speaks to us, and us only, and says that a situation is wrong, an injustice has been committed, and we must do something to reverse it. Here, we are in the realm of the mysterious, and in trying to suggest what causes us to act, it would be prudent to exercise a little humility, especially since so many of the challenges that confront us as a species are due to our arrogant belief that we know enough not to worry about the consequences of our actions.

We all want to be appreciated for what we do and the service we provide. We would all like to believe that the changes we advocate will be embraced immediately and that that change would be effortless. If we're lucky, the seeds we plant will germinate and grow, which is an added bonus we can continue to enjoy and be encouraged by. But genuine change is rarely easy. Quite often, our work is a struggle.

When we find ourselves becoming despondent about the

lack of success of our efforts, we can recall Jesus' parable of the mustard seed. Jesus describes the kingdom of heaven as a mustard seed that starts very small, but then grows into an enormous bush (see Matt. 13:31–32). The parable reminds us that it may take many months or years for anything like a shoot to appear. The climate for an idea's reception may be inhospitable, and it may require time for the idea to bury itself in the soil of the community to germinate and spread its roots. But, finally, the idea springs to life and begins to grow.

Of course, one doesn't stop when the first signs of life appear; indeed, that may be when the idea is most vulnerable to sudden changes in temperature, or to be scorched by the heat or drowned by the water of those who like nothing more than to stop new ideas from spreading. So it needs to be protected and nurtured. In the end, the idea can be so solidly grounded and so widely held that it supports other ideas that can flourish and grow, and is so large and dominant that everyone forgets what the landscape of society looked like before it appeared. Before then, however, activists need to remind themselves that it may be years before the fruits of their labor are seen. So the primary satisfaction has to come from the fact that you tried—that you served.

Another parable that can give one strength is that of the sower (see Matt. 13:1–23). It illustrates that society is made up of different people with different levels of receptivity. The sower throws his seeds at random: some fall on the path, and the birds eat them; some fall on rocky ground, where there is little soil in which they can germinate, and the sun scorches them and they die; some fall among thorns, which choke the seedlings. Some, however, fall on deep, fertile soil, where they can settle and grow.

We can look at the parable as an examination of how people experience new information. Some individuals are deaf to change or are distracted; as a result, new ideas or a new awareness has no way to embed itself in their consciousness. Some grasp the fact or idea initially, but are easily put off by the challenges that may arise in embracing it; they may not want to go against the wishes of their neighbors, or those in power, so the idea dies with them. However, some not only embrace the idea but have the courage of their convictions to see it through. They summon the values required.

These two parables remind us that ideas take time to flourish and that not everyone will receive your message. But they don't describe the tenacity that all of us who are working to replenish the earth need to have in the face of that indifference. When I want to remind myself of the effort we must expend, I think of the hummingbird. This might seem peculiar, since most of us think of the hummingbird as a tiny, delicate creature, skittish and elusive. But the story of the hummingbird first told to me by Professor Suji in Japan suggests a very different interpretation.

The story starts with an enormous fire, which breaks out and rages through the forest. All the animals, both big and small, flee to the forest edge to watch the conflagration—all, that is, except a hummingbird. "I will do something about this fire!" says the tiny bird. So it flies to the nearest stream and dives beneath the surface. Rising into the air, it carries a bead of water in its beak that it releases over the flames. The fire is huge, but over and over, the hummingbird flies to the stream, returns with a droplet in its beak, and lets it fall onto the flames. Each time, the bird believes that this one drop might make the difference.

While this is happening, the other animals—some with long trunks and large mouths like the elephant, giraffe, lion, and leopard—laugh at the diminutive creature. "What do you think you're doing?" they jeer. "You're only a hummingbird. You can see how big the forest fire is. Do you think you're going to do any good at all?" Without wasting any time and tired of their discouraging words and inaction, the hummingbird turns to the other animals as it prepares to fly back to the river, and says, "Well, I'm doing the best I can!"

On the face of it, of course, it's absurd that a tiny hummingbird carrying a few droplets of water in its beak would have any effect on a huge forest fire. Naturally, that's not the point of the story. The lessons we could take are these: that the hummingbird is working to its admittedly limited maximal capacity for the greater good of all the other animals and the forest. If the other, larger animals contributed to the effort, then the effect would be magnified. But they are too busy either laughing at the hummingbird's contribution or crying in despair to do their part. Their inertia only magnifies the hummingbird's effort. Of course, the larger moral of the story is that nothing is achieved unless one makes an effort. As the maxim attributed to the Chinese Daoist master Laozi states: "A journey of a thousand miles begins with a single step."

It may be true that the situation is hopeless and the hummingbird itself would never be able to quench the fire. It may also be the case that even if all the animals worked in concert with the hummingbird they wouldn't be able to extinguish all of the flames, either. But they may be able to stop *some* of the fire and therefore reduce its devastation of their home; and what is absolutely certain is that they won't know unless they try. Even if the hummingbird falls short of its ultimate goal, it can say again: "I'm doing the best I can."

So often we look at the task ahead of us and think we have neither sufficient agency nor ability. Especially when we consider the enormous challenges that await us in attempting to curb the potentially catastrophic effects of poverty, injustice, deforestation, desertification, soil loss, and climate change; or encouraging the disempowered to stand up for their rights and take responsibility for their own welfare; or demanding justice and fairness from our leaders. We feel too small, too insignificant, and too vulnerable; we fear that any effort will make us appear ridiculous if we try to bring about change. But, like the hummingbird, we must learn to persist, remain committed, and be patient.

Hummingbirds though we may feel ourselves to be, we nevertheless have to take our small beaks and carry that bead of water (that droplet of change) to where it is needed, and do it over and over again, notwithstanding the overwhelming odds. We may invite scorn or ridicule or indifference from those more powerful than us. Alternatively, however, we may encourage others to step forward and join us. We will never know until we leave a fixed state and give ourselves the energy to move into action. In the end, all we are called to do is the best we can.

This is an age-old story, but it's no less radical and no less hard for being so. It means giving your all, in the face of mockery and dejection, and tuning out the naysayers and critics. It suggests no more throwing up your arms in horror and despair; it demands making a commitment to run (or fly, if you're a hummingbird!) toward a problem rather than burying your head in the sand or fleeing as far as possible, falsely believing that you can escape it altogether. For it is unlikely that, given the effects of climate change, any wall will be high enough, any trench deep enough, any region remote enough, or any enclave rich enough, to fully withstand every hurricane, flood, drought, earthquake, or spreading desert.

There will be moments when you will become discouraged and disheartened. Committing yourself to be of service can be emotionally and spiritually taxing. The depth of the entrenched patterns and attitudes that hold back social development, and the refusal of human beings to protect their long-term interests over short-term gain and greed, can leave one feeling debilitated and drained. When the sapele tree fell in the Congo forest, for instance, I was also reminded of how burdensome it can sometimes be when you know what is being lost; you become dissatisfied with your own limitations and the indifference of others, and frustrated that more progress is not being made.

Not only is it exceptionally hard to continue our work with equanimity and focus when we face apathy from those we wish to mobilize. It's also very difficult when we're confronted with violence—whether to individuals or to the earth. We feel frustrated because what is being done is the opposite of what is good, fair, and just from our perspective. When we see values such as gratitude or love for the environment being violated or ignored, we become angry. In some ways, emotions such as anger and frustration are useful, because if you aren't agitated or unsettled then you're unlikely to want to do something about a situation. They can sometimes produce the energy that makes it possible to take action to alter unacceptable behavior—or stanch one of the earth's wounds—even though we may have to explain to others what we're so upset about. It is in such spirit that Jesus threw the moneychangers from the Temple.

Over the past few decades, some environmentalists have felt the threat to forests or other species or oceans or poor people's land and livelihoods to be so dire that they have gone beyond the nonviolent forms of protest used by activists such as Julia Butterfly Hill or those involved in the Chipko movement. Because resorting to violence may be tempting, I believe it's always worth asking yourself as an activist what you would consider to be an acceptable victory in your campaign, and whether your strategy is likely to bolster support for your movement or increase the strength of the opposition.

In addition to being honest about our motivations as agents of change, we have to recognize that in serving others and attempting to replenish the natural world, we cannot let our minds be shrouded by romantic notions of what it means to live sustainably. No matter how deeply we wish it, we cannot return to some mythical golden age when human beings were wholly connected to the life processes of the seasons and our sense of the divine was as immediate as it is portrayed in

Genesis. It's perhaps in the nature of the human being that we always imagine the times of our childhood, just as we may imagine the societies of the past, to be simpler, truer, and more authentic than the ones in which we have grown old.

Nor is it enough to believe that we can easily reverse the processes whereby everyone volunteers to live with fewer material possessions and create less waste. Not just our increasingly integrated and globalizing economies, but what appears to be our imagination itself have been geared to having more and throwing away and forgetting what we no longer want. In spite of the emergence of E. F. Schumacher's galvanizing concept that "small is beautiful" in the 1970s, we still determine our success on a personal and macroeconomic level by accumulating more.

When I learn that something isn't right, I have a tendency to search for a solution, as I did all those years ago with the women who inspired me to initiate the Green Belt Movement. My final piece of advice is very practical: look at the problem in front of you and try to solve it. Don't peer too far down the road and ask, "What can I do then?" for you risk being overwhelmed. I firmly believe that most problems we encounter have a solution. Although a day may arrive when you come across a problem you cannot address, most of them you will be able to make a contribution to solving.

Of course, you'll experience times when you feel you haven't done enough and that your work remains incomplete. As we grow older, we see our limitations with regard to time and energy. When we are young, it seems as if we have all the time in the world. If my work with the Green Belt Movement had evolved as I had hoped, tree-planting would be a national activity throughout Africa, people would be required to plant a certain number of trees on their land, soil erosion would be a thing of the past, and environmental education would be taught in every African school.

However, this hasn't happened, and now we face not only the mammoth difficulties that existed thirty years ago but still others (such as global warming) that we didn't foresee. If only I had fifty more years, I sometimes think, I could do so much, because now I know what to do—and there are so many more problems to be solved! But life isn't like that. Sometimes you don't have enough time, and too much needs to be done. I have come to accept that you cannot do everything, and no one should expect you to—including yourself.

We all live in different environments, with their own challenges and opportunities to create meaningful change. Our cultures and religious backgrounds may be different, and you may cherish different values. My aim is not to dictate how you should react to your circumstances, but to inspire you to use your own tradition's principles and culture to make a difference and heal Earth's wounds.

If I had one piece of advice for young people, it would be that it's important not to waste time—particularly because you think there are many years ahead. Don't fret about looking around to find the absolutely right vocation. Yes, you can try different careers or areas of interest, but you shouldn't waste the individual gifts you've been given or fall into damaging patterns, such as taking drugs or drinking too much alcohol. Your health is your best investment.

Ultimately, I would advise young people to let their

experiences take them to the next level, and always give 100 percent. That way, when you're old and look back, you can tell yourself that you may not have achieved all you set out to accomplish, but at least you tried your best. You were a hummingbird.

The work goes on. In recent years, the Green Belt Movement has sought to encourage wider adoption of the spiritual values that guide our work. For example, we are sharing our experience with grassroots environmental organizations across sub-Saharan Africa, through the Pan-African Green Belt Network, and outside of the African continent as well.

Writing this book has been a part of the process of sharing these values. The other, equally exciting initiative is the establishment of the Wangari Maathai Institute for Peace and Environmental Studies at the University of Nairobi. Its mission is:

> To transfer knowledge and skills on sustainable use of natural resources from academic halls and laboratories to the citizenry in villages and rural communities throughout Africa and beyond. And, in doing so, encourage transformational leadership grounded and focused on improving people's livelihoods and sharing cultures of peace.

At the institute, young people from Africa and other regions will be able to study the GBM's methodology and experience its work firsthand. In the process, I hope they will embrace the values at the center of this work. Then I envision them taking everything they have learned to their own grassroots organizations and applying it there. The institute will also foster interdisciplinary research and dialogue on the sustainable use of natural resources and community adaptation to climate change.

This task took on new urgency in 2009, when I became a grandmother to Ruth Wangari. When I look at my little granddaughter, born into an uncertain world, I wonder what the planet will look like when she is my age. Like all other infants, she is utterly dependent on the decisions we make to replenish the earth, or not. In our hands lie whether she and the millions of other babies will flourish on this small, blue sphere, along with the children and grandchildren of other species. I'm haunted by the possibility that she and the generation she belongs to will look back in deep disappointment and anger at our individual and collective failure to do enough, at how we turned away from difficult decisions because of a lack of personal or political will, or because we put profit over nonmaterial value.

"Where did they think we were going to live?" I fear they will ask of us. "What water did they imagine we'd be able to drink? What air to breathe? What food to eat? How did they calculate that we would be able to survive without the forests or the wetlands? Yet they slashed and burned and ignored all the signs. *Why did they do those things?*"

In the end, as this book has argued, the questions of how or whether we will heal Earth's wounds are spiritual ones: If we are fortunate enough to have all these possessions, what *then*? Are we happier, more fulfilled? Is our time spent fruitfully? Are we living a life that, if not examined, is nonetheless all we had hoped it would be? Or are we, in the end, simply feeding our craving—and in the process destroying the very life systems that sustain all of those material goods that we are so keen on buying?

To that extent, echoing Commander Collins, we might ask ourselves, *Why do we do what we do?* At its most basic, the answer might be that as living beings our task is to perpetuate our species. However, one might also speculate that the purpose of life can be found in family, and ready access to food, shelter, and community. Perhaps some might answer that our task is to accumulate as many possessions and as much wealth as possible, but I think they would be in the great minority.

At another level, one might consider one's purpose to be fulfilled in having left one's mark in some way through a positive contribution to the cultural, political, economic, or social fabric of one's community or nation, or in leaving the world a little more peaceful, healthier, and richer in biotic life than when we entered it. If most of us believe that the value of our lives is located outside materialism and that true wealth is not found only through monetary riches, then that should both make us revise any assumption we might have that conservation will necessarily mean deprivation and encourage us to act to preserve and repair what we have.

I believe that we need to rediscover our common experience with other creatures on Earth, and recognize that we have gone through an evolutionary process with them. They may not look like us, with their wings and scales and fur. We might like some; others, like mosquitoes, we may detest. But they are part of the process of life beginning and being sustained on this planet. An apt analogy is Noah in Genesis, who found a pair of each species and two by two placed them into his ark, mosquitoes and reptiles among them. Noah was not commanded to pick only those that were useful to him; he sheltered them all. God recognized that they are part of us; they needed the chance to survive, as well. And in giving them this chance, God gave us a chance, too. Now we must give that chance back to ourselves, and replenish the earth.

Acknowledgments

I would like to thank Mia MacDonald of Brighter Green and Martin Rowe of Lantern Books for their skill, thoughtfulness, and diligence in collaborating with me on *Replenishing the Earth*. I would also like to thank my editor, Trace Murphy, for his enthusiasm and commitment to the ideas explored here.

Over the years, I have had the great good fortune to learn from many people of faith and conviction who have expanded my consciousness. They have offered thought-provoking ideas about the mystery of our existence on this planet, and have engaged in practical activities to make Earth a greener, better place in which to live. Among these are the Consolata, Loreto, and Benedictine sisters and priests who were involved in my early education, as well as inspiring teachers of non-Christian faiths. I have also had the privilege of working with men and women with great spiritual depth and generosity. Among them, too many to mention by name, I would like to acknowledge: Steven Rockefeller, and the many extraordinary people involved in the creation and dissemination of the Earth Charter; Sr. Joan Kirby, Alison van Dyk, Mary Davidson, and my many friends at the Temple of Understanding; the late Thomas Berry; professors Mary Evelyn Tucker and John Grim, whose many books and conferences under the auspices of the Harvard Center for the Study of the World's Religions and the Forum on Religion and Ecology have been a revelation to many of us working at the intersection of both disciplines; former U.S.

vice president Al Gore, who has been a strong supporter of the Green Belt Movement; James "Gus" Speth, former dean of the Yale School of Forestry and Environmental Studies; and my friend the poet and writer Terry Tempest Williams.

Much of what we know about the history of the Kikuyu people before the arrival of British colonial forces and the missionaries in the latter half of the nineteenth century we owe to the work of Louis Leakey, the famous paleoanthropologist. His monumental three-volume *The Southern Kikuyu before 1903*, which remained unfinished at his death, was compiled, organized, and edited by his wife, Mary, and a number of others (including a botanist) and published by Academic Press of New York and London in 1977. His book was invaluable in the creation of this one.

Much appreciation goes to my many friends in Japan, especially at Mainichi Newspapers Co., which introduced the Green Belt Movement to Japan and became a most reliable partner in the mottainai campaign, led by Kazuyoshi Sanada. A devoted network of friends was created, especially through the Itochu Corporation, whose associates support the work of the Green Belt Movement.

I've also been inspired by the many individuals, including members of the Green Belt Movement family, with whom I work very closely. While they are too numerous to mention by name, their spirit has been indispensable to the movement's work both in Kenya and around the world. There are many others who, in the course of years, have entrusted us with the financial resources to continue the movement's ever-expanding work. To all of them, I am deeply grateful.

Nothing that I have written in *Replenishing the Earth* would have been possible—in every sense of the word—without my family. My mother was a woman whose natural reverence combined with her practical good sense meant that she cared for and nurtured creation, and showed me how to work with the land. My children and grandchild continue to be a source of great inspiration and support in all my efforts. I am deeply indebted to them.

Notes

All URLs accessed April 2, 2010.

INTRODUCTION

1. S. Soloman, et al., eds., "Summary for Policymakers" in *Contribution of Working Group I to the Fourth Assessment Report of the Intergovernmental Panel on Climate Change, 2007*, (Cambridge, UK, and New York: Cambridge University Press, 2007), 1–18.

2. James J. McCarthy, et al., eds., "Africa," chap. 10 in *Contribution of Working Group II to the Intergovernmental Panel on Climate Change, 2001*, (Cambridge, UK, and New York: Cambridge University Press, 2001), 488–531.

CHAPTER THREE:
CHANGING PERSPECTIVES

1. Quoted in "Space Photography: The Eyes of an Astronaut," by Frank Bures, *Audubon* (January–February 2006), Vol. 108, No. 1, www.audubonmagazine.org/fieldnotes/fieldnotes0601 .html#astronaut, and redacted in *The Independent* (August 11, 2005), http://www.independent.co.uk/opinion/commentators/ eileen-collins-from-space-the-earths-atmosphere-looks-like- an-eggshell-502306.html.

2. Quotations taken from http://spacequotations.com/earth .html, Kevin W. Kelley, ed., *The Home Planet* (New York: Addison-Wesley, 1988), and "Astronauts," *Encyclopedia of Religion and Nature* (see chapter 4, note 1).

3. James Ratemo, "Disaster Looms in Turkana as Drought Persists," *The Standard* (March 31, 2005); "Droughts of the Recent Past," in Turkana-History, www.bluegecko.org/kenya/ tribes/turkana/history.htm#drought.

4.   Kerry Kriger, "The Disappearance of Frogs: Why We Should
     Be Very Worried," August 6, 2009, http://ecohearth.com.

CHAPTER FOUR:
THE POWER OF THE TREE

1.   Information about the social and religious uses of the tree is
     referenced from many articles in the *Encyclopedia of Religion and
     Nature,* edited by Bron Taylor (New York: Continuum, 2005).
     Also included is information from *The Encyclopedia of Religion,*
     Second Edition, edited by Lindsay Jones (Farmington Hills,
     Mich.: Macmillan), pp. 9333–40. Also sourced are *The Oxford
     Handbook of Religion and Ecology,* edited by Roger S. Gottlieb
     (New York: Oxford University Press, 2006), and *This Sacred
     Earth: Religion, Nature, Environment,* edited by Roger S. Gott-
     lieb (New York: Routledge, 1996).

2.   "In the Shade of the Banyan Tree," *The Economist,* April 8,
     2009.

3.   Robert Costanza, et al. "The Value of the World's Ecosystem
     Services and Natural Capital," sourced from the website of the
     University of Vermont's Gund Institute for Ecological Eco-
     nomics, www.uvm.edu/giee/publications/Nature_Paper.pdf.

4.   UN Environment Programme, *TEEB — The Economics of Eco-
     systems and Biodiversity [TEEB] for National and International
     Policy Makers — Summary: Responding to the Value of Nature,*
     2009, and press release, "TEEB report released on the Eco-
     nomics of Ecosystems and Biodiversity for National and In-
     ternational Policy Makers," November 13, 2009.

CHAPTER FIVE:
SACRED GROVES, SACRED NO MORE

1.   Christine Downing, *The Goddess: Mythological Images of the
     Feminine* (New York: Crossroad Publishing Company, 1981),
     pp. 13–16; Steve Davis, "The Canaanite-Hebrew Goddess,"

in *The Book of the Goddess Past and Present*, Carl Olson, ed. (New York: Crossroad Publishing Company, 1992), pp. 68–79; Susan Ackerman, "Asherah/Asherim" in The Jewish Women's Archive, http://jwa.org/encyclopedia/article/asherahasherim -bible; David Leeming, *Jealous Gods & Chosen People: The Mythology of the Middle East* (New York: Oxford University Press, 2004), p. 94.

2. Information about the Chipko movement gathered from Wikipedia, http://en.wikipedia.org/wiki/Chipko_movement.

3. Himachal Pradesh, IANS, "New Chipko Movement: Himachal Women Tie Rakhis to Protect Trees," *Deccan Herald*, August 3, 2009.

4. The speech can be read in its entirety at www.rightlivelihood .org/chipko_speech.html.

5. Julia Butterfly Hill, *The Legacy of Luna: The Story of a Tree, a Woman and the Struggle to Save the Redwoods* (San Francisco: HarperOne, 2001), p. 123.

CHAPTER SIX:
GRATITUDE AND RESPECT

1. Olivia Zaleski, "China's Plastic Bag Ban Will Save 37 Million Barrels of Oil," The Daily Green, www.dailygreen.com, September 1, 2008.

2. Yvonne Chan, "China Saves 40 Million Plastic Bags," www .businessgreen.com, May 26, 2009.

3. For information on Japan's forest cover, see http://rainforests .mongabay.com/deforestation/2000/Japan.htm; for wood consumption in Japan, see Wood Resource Quarterly Press Release, June 29, 2009, www.free-press-release.com/news/ 200906/1246300953.html; for use of chopsticks in Japan, see Jiro Taylor, "The Waribashi Conundrum: Disposable Chopsticks," in Japan Visitor, www.japanvisitor.com/index .php?cID=361&pID=375.

4. I am grateful to friends for reminding me of these Jewish mandates.

5. See www.recyclingconsortium.org.uk/schools/christmas_waste .htm.

CHAPTER NINE:
THE COMMITMENT TO SERVICE

1. The second quotation is from Thomas Berry, *The Great Work: One Way into the Future* (New York: Bell Tower, 1999), p. 115.

2. Leonardo Boff, *Ecology and Liberation* (Maryknoll, N.Y.: Orbis, 1996), p. 25, in *The Oxford Handbook of Religion and Ecology,* Roger S. Gottlieb, ed. (New York: Oxford University Press), p. 80. For more on liberation theology as applied to ecology, see *Handbook,* pp. 516–20.

CHAPTER TEN:
SPIRITUALITY MEETS ACTIVISM

1. Drawn from the biography page on a website dedicated to Thomas Berry, written by Mary Evelyn Tucker, at www .thomasberry.org/Biography/tucker-bio.html.

About the Author

Wangari Muta Maathai was born in Nyeri, Kenya, in 1940. The Nobel Peace Prize laureate of 2004, she has three grown children and one grandchild, and lives and works in Nairobi.

My life's work has evolved into much more than planting trees. By planting trees, my colleagues and I in the Green Belt Movement planted ideas. Like trees, these ideas grew. By providing education, access to water, and equity, the Green Belt Movement empowers people—most of them poor and most of them women—to take action, directly improving the lives of individuals and families.

Our experience of more than thirty years has also shown that simple acts can lead to great change and to respect for the environment, good governance, and cultures of peace. Such change is not limited to Kenya, or Africa. The challenges facing Africa, particularly the degradation of the environment, are facing the entire world. Only by working together can we hope to solve some of the problems of this precious planet. It is my fervent wish that you will seek to learn more about the work of the Green Belt Movement by visiting our website, www.greenbeltmovement.org. Please share in our message of hope.

—Wangari Maathai